W9-BNL-095

THE SHAPING OF A CHRISTIAN FAMILY

Other books by the same author

Through Gates of Splendor
Shadow of the Almighty
The Savage My Kinsman
No Graven Image
These Strange Ashes
The Liberty of Obedience
Let Me Be a Woman
Love Has a Price Tag
The Journals of Jim Elliot
The Mark of a Man
Discipline: The Glad Surrender
Passion and Purity
A Lamp For My Feet
A Chance to Die
Loneliness
On Asking God Why
All That Was Ever Ours
A Path Through Suffering

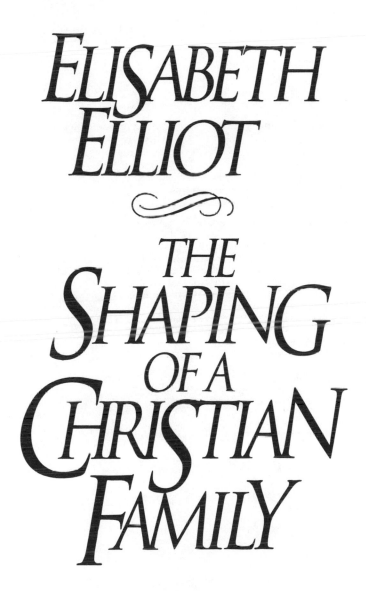

ELISABETH ELLIOT

THE SHAPING OF A CHRISTIAN FAMILY

OLIVER NELSON

THOMAS NELSON PUBLISHERS
NASHVILLE

Published in Nashville, Tennessee, by Oliver-Nelson Books, a division of Thomas Nelson, Inc.

Scripture quotations marked NIV are taken from the HOLY BIBLE: NEW INTERNA-TIONAL VERSION. Copyright © 1973, 1978, 1984 by the International Bible Society. Used by permission of Zondervan Bible Publishers. Scripture quotations noted RSV are from the Revised Standard Version of the Bible, copyrighted 1946, 1952, © 1971, 1973. Scripture quotations noted JB are from THE JERUSALEM BIBLE, copyright © 1966 by Darton, Longman & Todd Ltd. and Doubleday & Company, Inc. Used by permission. Scripture quotations noted NEB are from *The New English Bible.* © The Delegates of the Oxford University Press 1961, 1970. Reprinted by permission. Scripture quotations noted PHILLIPS are from J. B. Phillips: THE NEW TESTAMENT IN MODERN ENGLISH, Revised Edition. © J. B. Phillips 1958, 1960, 1972. Used by permission of Macmillan Publishing Co., Inc. Scripture quotations noted AV are from The King James Version of the Holy Bible.

Printed in the United States.

Library of Congress Cataloging-in-Publication Data

Elliot, Elisabeth.
    The shaping of a Christian family / Elisabeth Elliot.
        p.   cm.
    ISBN 0-8407-9136-4
    1. Family—Religious   life.   2. Parenting—Religious   aspects—Christianity.
    3. Howard family.   I. Title.
    BV4526.2E45   1992
    248.8'45'0922—dc20   91-45214
                                                                        CIP

        4   5   6   7 — 96   95   94

With love

to

Phil, Dave, Ginny, Tom, and Jim
heirs with me to the inestimable legacy
of the home I have tried to describe

❦

*Love the LORD
your God with all your heart and with all
your soul and with all your strength.
These commandments that I give you today
are to be upon your hearts.
Impress them on your children.
Talk about them when you sit at home and when you walk
along the road, when you lie down
and when you get up.*

DEUTERONOMY 6:5–7 NIV

*The spirit of faith and piety
of the parents should be regarded as the most
powerful means for the preservation, upbringing,
and strengthening of the life
of grace in children.*

THEOPHAN THE RECLUSE

CONTENTS

Introduction

When my mother was seventy-nine years old she was asked to write an article for *Moody Monthly* on training children. Her perspectives as described here seem the best introduction to the story of our family.

Teaching Your Toddler

by Katharine G. Howard

A SMALL BATTLE of wills took place between my firstborn son and me. Breakfast was over for his daddy and me. But sitting in his highchair, Phil dawdled with the remains of his milk. He announced firmly, "Wanna git down."

"Just finish your milk, then you can get down," I told him, not dreaming that this was a crisis.

He sat quietly for a time, then declared, "Wanna git down."

"Yes, as soon as you finish your milk." We repeated this scene every few minutes for more than an hour. I began to realize that my authority was being tested. Inwardly I determined that he would sit there until he did what I told him. Just how long that would have taken had it not been for the milkman, I do not know. Phil loved to watch the milkman come down the cobblestone street in our suburb of Schaerbeek in Brussels, Belgium, with his little cart pulled by his dog. When Phil heard him coming, down went the milk and he wormed his way out of the highchair in no time.

Years later, during his military service, Phil wrote his father and me thanking us for teaching him obedience. It never occurred to him to disobey an order, he said, but many men tried to get around doing what they were told and consequently they spent a lot of time in the brig. "Train up a child in the way he should go and when he is old he will not depart from it" is as true today as when Solomon wrote it several thousand years ago. Running one's eye down the columns of any concordance on the words *obey*, *obedience*, and *obedient* gives some idea of the importance of these words in God's sight. "Behold, to obey is better than sacrifice, and to hearken than the fat of rams," Samuel told Saul. In order to properly *hearken*, which is the beginning of learning, one must be obedient.

Training must come before teaching. Before parents can train their children properly, they must first discipline themselves. An orderly home and orderly habits can be accomplished only by agreeing together on these things. Our home ran on a tight schedule. My husband had to catch his commuter train on time, and each child had to finish his duties and leave for school on time. My husband insisted on a leisurely breakfast and family prayers. This is impossible unless the children cooperate. And they don't cooperate unless they are disciplined from their earliest days. This discipline lays the groundwork for teaching.

Praying together for wisdom and standing together on all matters of discipline should be a rule for parents. Older children quickly notice when they can play one parent against the other: "If Mommy won't let me go, I'll ask Daddy. He won't know that Mommy has said no." Parents of young children (and older ones, too, of course) should read the book of Proverbs frequently and soak up the wisdom given by the Spirit of God.

❦

Aren't toddlers too young for serious training? Years ago when our three older children were quite small, my husband and I invited to our home a father of ten children, all of whom had become fine Christian men and women. When we had our three tucked safely into bed, we young parents began to ply our guest with questions on child-training. I have never forgotten one thing he said: "If you don't get obedience by the time they are eighteen months old, it is too late!"

I would hardly say eighteen months is too late to teach a child obedience, but certainly it becomes harder the longer a child is left in doubt as to who is in authority. We hear much these days about not frustrating the child by saying "don't." Actually the real frustration comes when he has been naughty and then is not punished. I noticed so often that a speedy application of a switch to little legs cleared the atmosphere. For weeks to come there was no need for further chastisement. We are told that "whom the Lord loveth He chasteneth." Unless we follow His example firmly and consistently, are we truly loving our children?

As each of our six became eighteen months old, I found that our wise friend had been correct. When the child begins to crawl and then to toddle, he puts his parents to the test. "Does Mommy *really* mean don't touch?" he seems to wonder. "I'll just try her out and see!" And he does just that.

I recall watching my son Dave as his little son Michael edged toward my gas stove in our kitchen in Florida. He had been pulled away from it and told not to turn on the gas jets. Yet he edged slowly toward the stove, stopping now and then to look at his father who continued to say quietly, "Michael, don't touch that." When Michael touched, he found out that Daddy meant what he said. There were hot tears as a result.

Even tiny babies can be taught when put to bed that crying does no good. The mother must discipline herself. If she is sure that the baby is dry and warm and has a full tummy, then she must let him cry. It only takes a few nights for him to learn that it is a waste of time. The tantrum-throwing toddler can be dealt with easily by relegating him to a room by himself. Crying and screaming aren't much fun without an audience.

There is a great deal of talk these days about having things *unstructured*. Just how can a Christian make this jibe with such Scriptures as "Let everything be done decently and in order" (I Cor. 14:40), or with a careful study of God's creation? What would happen to the galaxies if they were un-structured? Certainly there should be order in the home. Structure in a home includes more than scheduling. It means teaching a child to discipline his mind. Even a small child can learn to pay attention and to look at his parent when the parent is speaking to him. During our family prayers, we allowed no playing or mind wandering. We expected our children to listen.

🍂

Training of a child begins early, but when can we begin to *teach* him? What greater joy for a mother than a low rocking chair and a wee baby in her arms to sing to? Let his little ears hear her sing "Jesus Loves Me" or "Away in a Manger" or "Savior, Like a Shepherd Lead Us." The rocking rhythm auto-matically gets songs and verses into a child's mind. Soothed by the motion and his mother's love, he is more open and can learn without effort.

An appreciation of good literature can be instilled early. *Peter Rabbit* and *Benjamin Bunny, Squirrel Nutkin* and *Jeremy Fisher* soon became friends of our children. They also loved the catchy swing of the poems by A. A. Milne. And we wore out two Bible story books.

My husband instituted family prayers as soon as we were married. Immediately after breakfast we had a hymn, a brief Bible reading, a prayer committing each member of the fam-ily to God's care and then we united in saying the Lord's prayer. When the children were little, I held them on my lap while my husband played the piano for the hymn. I would hold baby Jim's arms and help him beat time to the music. Soon he did it on his own.

I found that simply repeating Psalm 23 each night to Jim after he was tucked in bed was a painless way of implanting this beautiful song of David in his heart and mind. Within a week he was beginning to say it with me, and it was part of the going-to-bed ritual. As he mastered Psalm 23, we added other Scripture.

In teaching young children, it is well to remember the words in Isaiah 28:10, "For precept must be upon precept,

precept upon precept, line upon line, line upon line, here a little and there a little." It is thus our patient God has dealt with us; and so we must deal with our little ones, repeating often the Word of God so that it will be hidden in their hearts so they will "not sin against God."

We noticed that the repetition of the Lord's prayer at the end of family worship was an easy way to learn it. My small grandson, Charles, wanted to join in on it but had not mastered it all. However, he came out good and strong on what he did know. In clear tones he would say, "heaven . . . name . . . come . . . done . . ." "Trespasses" was somewhat of a stumper, but in time he had that down pat too and soon could join in the whole prayer.

The old rendering of Psalm 127:3 as given in the *Book of Common Prayer* challenges every parent: "Lo, children and the fruit of the womb are an heritage and gift that cometh of the Lord." How are we cherishing this gift? No time spent in this responsibility is lost.

> "We give Thee but Thine own,
> Whate'er the gift may be:
> All that we have is Thine alone,
> A trust, O Lord, from Thee."
> (W. W. How)

Let's live before our children that they may be able to truly honor us as it says in Ephesians 6:2, "Honor thy father and mother; which is the first commandment with promise."

Very young children are capable of giving their hearts to Christ. One of my sons has no recollection of when this took place in his life, but he knows it did. My younger daughter recalls when at age four she and I knelt by my bed and she asked the Lord Jesus to come into her heart. She says she has never doubted her salvation since then. Remember the loving invitation of the Lord, "Suffer the little children to come unto Me and forbid them not, for of such is the kingdom of heaven" (Matt. 19:14).

God grant that none of our little ones will have to say in later life the sad words from Proverbs 5:12-14 (Jerusalem Bible), "Alas, I hated discipline, my heart spurned correction; I would not hear the voice of my masters, I would not listen to those who tried to teach me. Now I am all but reduced to the depths of misery, in the presence of the whole community."

PREFACE

The upstairs front bedroom of the house where I spent most of the first nine years of my life was large and sunny, with a rocking chair in the bay window where Mother loved to sit to feed and rock her babies, to sing to us and tell us stories. We were three then—Philip, called Sonny at that time, I, Elisabeth, known as Bets to Mother and Betsy to Daddy, and David, who was Davy then.

My earliest memory is of sitting on Mother's lap, facing her, looking into her vivid blue eyes (they were very, very blue) and playing with a gold sunburst pin on the V-neck of her blue dress.

She sang "A Capital Ship," "Go Tell Aunt Nancy," "I Went to Visit a Friend One Day," "Bobby Shaftoe," "Mathilda Told Such Awful Lies," and "She's a Darling, She's a Daisy." Of the many gospel songs she sang I especially remember "There Is Sunshine in My Soul Today" and "Wonderful Words of Life." We loved to be read to from a series of books called *My Bookhouse,* and from A. A. Milne and Beatrix Potter. We loved the stories she made up about a little monkey called Jocko, but we begged most often to hear about "when you were a little girl."

When Mother reached her seventies I asked her to put the whole story into writing.

"Oh *pooh,*" she said. "*Who'd* ever want to read *that?*" (Mother could not talk without italics. I think I picked up her habit.)

"All of us," I said, meaning the six of us and our husbands

and wives and children and grandchildren and who knew how many more generations.

Argument convinced her there would certainly be some readers. After all, I pointed out, what generation in the history of mankind had seen the cataclysmic changes in technology and society that her generation had seen—from bone china to Styrofoam, from linsey-woolsey to double-knit synthetics, from china washbasins and tin tubs to Jacuzzis, from kerosene and gas lamps to electricity, from the horse and buggy to the jet plane?

"Oh *mercy!*" she said. "*I* wouldn't know what to say. *I'm* no writer. *You* do it."

"Get yourself a looseleaf notebook," I told her, "and start putting things down as they come to mind, one vignette per page, so you can insert things later that you've forgotten. Take your time."

She did it. She got carried away with the project, spent ten years on it, even pasted in photographs, and ended up with two fat volumes.

This, then, and not my childhood recollection of those stories, has been my primary source for the facts and the chronology of our family life. Excerpts from Mother's story are printed in a different typeface, Tiffany, and set ragged right.

My father died at sixty-five. Alas, we had not thought of asking him to write his story. We very much wish we had. But we have the half-dozen books he wrote, the few years' worth of diaries he kept, some of his letters and letters written to my mother about him after he died, and we still have his sister Anne who is very good at answering questions.

❦

My parents' life stories are naturally of keen interest to me, but I had not thought of putting them into a book until a few years ago when I began to hear from many young fathers and mothers who earnestly desire to establish Christian homes but have no such background as I have. How does one go about it? What shape should it take? Where are the models worth copying?

I offer this story of *one* man's family. Some may want to

take it as a prescription for theirs, but I do not offer it as such. It is meant primarily to be a description of how *one* Christian couple went about ordering their own home. The Howards sought to learn and apply godly principles from the Bible, and those principles are worth reviewing often, though their application may differ in other homes. Our parents prayed every day for God's help. They made mistakes, and they asked His forgiveness and, on occasion, ours too.

The question will be raised: What about the products? What of the six Howard children? I speak for all when I say that we thank God for the home we grew up in. We loved our parents, and we knew they loved us. We respected them, and the principles they taught us certainly helped to shape the six homes we established when we married, as different as our spouses and our homes have been. I speak for myself when I say that I both bewildered and grieved my parents, no doubt far more often than I know, but their prayers followed me (surely they follow me still), and only Eternity will show how great is the debt I owe them.

Magnolia, Massachusetts, July 1991

CHAPTER 1

A
VICTORIAN
HOME

"Get your clothes on quickly, Tom. There's a surprise for you downstairs."

Uncle Tom was about ninety years old when he told us, his nieces and nephews, about that memorable morning in June 1899 when Granny Marshall, the old nurse, came in to wake him up.

The bicycle! Surely it would be the bicycle he had longed for. Almost everything he had was secondhand, well used by his older brother Frank. If only he could have just one wonderful, new, shiny thing.

He threw on shirt, knickers, black stockings, high buttoned shoes (no time to button them), and raced downstairs. Was ever an eight-year-old more desperately disappointed? Not a shiny bike but a small bundle in his mother's arms, a red squalling infant, of whose coming he had not been given even an inkling.

"Your baby sister, Tom," said his mother. "Her name is Katharine."

Katharine, my mother, was born to Frank and Ida Keen Gillingham on Clarkson Avenue in Germantown, a section of Philadelphia where her father was in the lumber business. Their large and comfortable house was one half of what was then called a "double" house, sharing one wall with the next-door neighbors. The first photograph of baby Katharine is one of those old blue-toned ones. It shows a lavishly upholstered wicker carriage with high wheels and a folded parasol. Surrounded by cushions and afghans sits a beautifully be-frilled and bonneted child with a round face and bright eyes.

Her autobiography tells the story:

     ﹏ Dr. Thomas Carmichael, father of the now well-known Leonard Carmichael [for many years head of the Smithsonian Institution], ushered my two brothers and me into the world in the house my father and mother moved into right after they were married.

     Granny Marshall, the nurse, is one of the first people I remember. ﹏

The widow of a sailor lost at sea, Granny spent a good deal of time making "handy sewing kits for seamen." When Katharine was three or four years old the old lady broke her leg. It was badly set and remained permanently stiff. "When she came to visit us, as she frequently did, it became my duty to help her put on her high black buttoned shoes and button them up with a button hook, a duty I never cared for!"

Another woman the little girl early learned to love was her "colored Mammy," Sarah Ann Hackley, who always wore a black dress with white collar and cuffs, a white apron, and a white cap. "The world came to an end (for a time) the day she left when I was about six. I remember sitting at the top of the long straight stairs and watching her go. I could not imagine life without her."

The house had an iron picket fence in front and a big porch with cane rocking chairs. In the front yard was "a small spinny of evergreen trees and in one of them was an arrangement of boughs that formed a nice place to sit. It was my own special hide-out and I loved it."

When you entered the front door you passed through a vestibule into a spacious front hall, then into the parlor on the right which held a huge, fat-legged player piano with paper music rolls. Pictures of this room show lamps with immense fringed shades, spindly-legged tables with tasseled velvet or lace covers, and ornate chairs covered with fringed plush, scattered about in what seems, a century later, a haphazard fashion which has little to do with present-day notions of comfort, convenience, or symmetry. Heavy gilt frames on the walls hold paintings of lovely ladies. On the mantel are cut glass vases, a chiming clock, candelabra with crystal prisms, the same things which later adorned the mantel I remember in our house. Back of this room was the den where the little girl would watch herself in a great pier glass as she danced to the music of the player piano. Then came the dining room with a swinging door into the kitchen where the cooking was done on a coal stove which had a hot water boiler attached. It was here that a tragedy took place when Katharine was about four.

෴ Mother was gay and full of fun. However, I believe she never fully recovered from the tragedy . . . Her sister, after being widowed, had decided to build a cottage at Belmar, New Jersey, to get away from the heat of the city in the summers. She had gone there to oversee the work and left her two little girls with Mother. I think they were ten and seven. Betty was the younger. We had just finished lunch and Mother wanted to go to the kitchen to speak to the maid. She told us three little girls to go upstairs. Betty, who was devoted to her, followed her out to the kitchen. Suddenly there was a terrific explosion. The boiler had exploded by the stove. A piece of metal struck Betty killing her instantly. Helen and I didn't know what had happened but we were herded quickly over to the house next door where we were put into the parlor and left there for what seemed hours. ෴

Upstairs was the sitting room. Here along with the horse-hair sofa and plush stuffed armchairs were Ida's beautiful Governor Winthrop desk (now in my guestroom), a tall telephone on the mantelpiece with its bells mounted on the wall above, and a "speaking tube," a sort of intercom into which one could blow to attract the cook's attention in the kitchen. Her father's smoking stand afforded the little girl pleasure, as he kept his cards and cribbage set there with its chips and little brass pins.

The parents' bedroom was at the front, with Katharine's

next to it. On the third floor were the brothers' bedroom and sitting room, a maid's room, and a storeroom.

✍ Housecleaning in those days was a formidable affair. Rugs had to be taken out in the back yard and a man hired to BEAT them with strong sticks, one in each hand, and if he had a proper sense of rhythm it was fun to hear him. To prepare for summer linen carpets were put down on top of the other carpets and all the furniture was swathed in huge linen covers, and the pictures covered with cheese cloth. ᕙ

In the broad back yard were a sandbox, a trellis covered with grapevines, and a wonderful cherry tree from which Katharine was allowed only a few cherries at a time, as they were not considered "good for little girls." The pens for Tom's chickens and Frank's pigeons were at the back of the yard. Neighborhood cats were interested in the penned chickens and pigeons, so Teddy, Katharine's "bulldog of sorts," was taught to chase them. "This caused me much heartache later on when I used to bring beautiful 'coon' cats home from Maine, hoping Teddy would learn to like them. He never did, and their nine lives were quickly used up under his attentions. One shake was all it took!"

Katharine and her beloved Teddy, born at about the same time, were inseparable. He felt as she did about many things, including the Fourth of July. Together they would retreat trembling under the bed to get away from the big "cannon crackers" Tom and Frank set off.

✍ Once I was sitting on the front porch in my little rocking bench. My mother had given me a small handful of shelled peanuts (another thing that little girls must not have too many of). Teddy came and sat in front of me drooling. He loved peanuts too. Suddenly I dropped one and before I could get it Teddy had swallowed it whole. I was beside myself. I was going to get it back or know the reason why. I stuck my hand into his mouth and tried to get it down his throat, all the while screaming loudly. Our postman was coming along on the other side of the street, and seeing me in that position dropped his bag and came running to my assistance, thinking poor Teddy was chewing my arm up. ☙

Teddy hated the iceman and made his life miserable growling and barking fiercely as he would come staggering into the back shed, lugging a huge block of perhaps fifty pounds of ice with his tongs. The icebox, "a coffin-shaped affair," had a large ice compartment with a hole in the bottom to allow the water to drip into a pan below. "Woe betide the maid who forgot to empty it once or twice a day! A trickle of water would announce the overflow of the pan." Katharine was always glad to see the iceman, however, for while the patient horse waited out front she was allowed to jump onto the back of his wagon and scoop up the ice shavings he had left after cutting the blocks with his pick.

There were few diversions for children in the early twentieth century, and one gets the distinct impression that they were happier because of it. Simple things which cost nothing provided sufficient entertainment, and the mischief Katharine and her friend Dorothy got into was fairly innocuous.

Next door lived old Mrs. Manship, a matriarch who had contrived to keep all of her grown children grouped around her—Horace, a stiff bachelor, and three spinster sisters, Dovey, Wheaty, and Browny, remote and unapproachable, all of them. Katharine and Dorothy, determined somehow to breach the silence, threw sand from the sandbox over the back fence into the Manship yard. There is no record of the consequences of the diversion this must have furnished the Manships. Perhaps they needed an interruption in their quiet life now and then.

Across the way was the big Wistar Estate, another impregnable citadel. "We were never allowed to go there, though I remember trying to sneak in and pick a few violets from under their trees in the spring."

☙ The Wistar farm was at the dead-end of the street and Old Billy, with his head bent forward in a permanent crook (someone said he had fallen off a hay wagon and broken his neck many years before) used to deliver milk from the farm. I remember being pop-eyed one winter day when he came into the kitchen and stood leaning his hand casually on the hot stove.

One morning I found on waking up that the Wistar barn had burned down during the night. I was furious that I had slept through all the excitement as the fire engines pulled by three horses galloped past our house and no one had wakened me.

On hot summer days the dust was thick in the street. We could look for the watering cart to come along to lay the dust for a brief time. This consisted of a sort of tank cart with a kind of sprinkler system turned on or off at the will of the driver.

One of the sounds I recall hearing was the cheerful tinkling of the little bell the scissors grinder used to let people know he was in the neighborhood. Then one could take him all the knives and scissors needing sharpening and watch him whirl his grindstone and see the sparks fly. ৵

CHAPTER 2

A
GOODLY
HERITAGE

~◎ **M**y brother Frank tells a story about our grandfather (Frank Clemens Gillingham) which he insists is true. Grandfather was an officer in the Union Army. When Lincoln was killed, his body was shipped by train to Springfield, Illinois. Grandfather was in charge of the funeral train, which made its slow, sad way west, stopping at almost every town on the way, in order that the people could have a last look at the great man. It fell to Grandfather's lot to see that the cinders from the engine were carefully brushed off Lincoln's face at each stop.

I remember in 1913 when my grandfather returned from attending the fiftieth anniversary of the Battle of Gettysburg. This occasion was attended by veterans of both armies, the Confederate and the Union. He told us that one day while there, he was walking along the road and saw an old man sitting by the side of the road and stopped to chat with him. The man asked him what regiment he had been in and when he was told he said to my grandfather, "Sir, I was your drummer boy."

He also told us how beautifully the battle field had been fixed up. My father spoke up and asked him if he had ever seen the battle field of Antietam—that he thought it very beautiful. My grandfather replied very quietly, "I fought there." I have read that it was the bloodiest battle of the bloodiest of wars. ⌒

Katharine's father was Frank Morris Gillingham, eldest son of this grandfather. He entered his father's lumber business while still in his teens.

⌒ Every morning, year in and year out, Dad would have the same breakfast—coffee, toast (I guess), and two boiled eggs opened into a big bowl with hashed brown potatoes put on top of them, which he mixed up in a jiffy for he was in a hurry to get his train on the Reading Railroad at Wistar Station, which was at the foot of a long hill on Wistar Street. Down the hill in the morning when he was fresh and rested, up the hill in the evening when he was hot and weary from a long day in the lumber yard. It must have been trying, but he came home to a cheerful, pretty little wife, five feet tall, Ida Keen. She was the youngest of four children of Alfred Keen. She had a brother Harry who was killed in a railroad accident, another brother Uncle Will, whom I vaguely remember as a tall, handsome man suffering from what I suppose was arthritis. Her sister, christened for some obscure reason Lizzie, whom some of you knew as Nana, was next in line, and then Mother, who I can sort of imagine was the pet of the family.

My only recollection of my Grandpa Keen is of him sitting in a big rocking chair at Aunt Lizzie's house where he lived, and sending Helen, Aunt Lizzie's oldest daughter, around to the store to get him some CHEWING tobacco!

My Grandfather and Grandmother Gillingham lived in a beautiful big house on the corner of Wayne Avenue and Coulter Street in Germantown. Living with them were her mother, my great-grandmother Tacy Shoemaker Morris, and Great-Grandmother's sister Mattie, a maiden lady of uncertain age and NOT very beautiful, as I recall. Great-Grandmother dressed in black with ruching at the neck and cuffs (see "ruche" in the dictionary). A small cap sat on her head and a little bang of false hair adorned her forehead. She sat on a low rocker by the window that looked out on Coulter Street and made those beautiful silk patchwork quilts that Bets has and also I think I gave one to Phyllis. You should study the infinite number of different kinds of stitching on them.

Grandmother (Tacy Morris Gillingham) died when I was quite small and I just barely remember her. One thing, though—when we were invited there for Sunday dinner we almost always had HOMINY GRITS, the big kind! I'm sure we had other good things, but as I didn't LIKE those big grits they are the one thing I remember! After she died her place was always set for dinner as though she were expected. This puzzled me very much.

For a short time we had a horse named Old Tom. He was about as broad as he was long and always shied at manholes, to the embarrassment of the occupants of the carriage. I remember two big buffalo robes and have a vague mental picture of being in a sleigh, tucked in with those huge things around me.

On hot summer days horses that pulled heavy carts and wagons were often fitted out with straw hats with holes in them for their ears to stick through, giving them a comical appearance. At intervals along the streets and out in the country were placed big tubs full of water to give the horses a drink. When it was time to feed them their driver would fasten a "feed bag" containing oats over their noses.

The first auto I remember belonged to our family doctor, Dr. Carmichael. It looked just like a buggy, big wheels and hard tires, no steering wheel but a sort of bar that crossed the lap of the driver. I have no idea what make it was. Maybe it was run by electricity.

My father bought a car, a Columbia, about 1904, I think. There were no doors, one just stepped in from a running board. The driver sat on the right side (a hangover from horse-and-buggy days, no doubt) with the wheel set at right angles to him and a horn with a rubber bulb that one squeezed. I don't remember whether or not those early models had curtains to be put on by hand in case of rain. One day I was riding up front with my father

—it must have been the Fourth of July for I had an American flag that I was waving gaily. Unfortunately I waved it in my father's face thus obstructing his view and we ended up against a street light or telephone pole. My father was not happy—neither was I!

It did seem we often ended our trips in a ditch, the roads then having very deep ditches on either side, and in order to avoid another vehicle one had to pull over a bit too far for comfort, and if the road was slippery the car gently slid into the ditch, making it very difficult to get out unless someone with a horse came along. Then we were subjected to the humiliation of hearing the bystanders sing out, "Honk, honk! Get a horse!"

For traveling in the open cars of the early nineteen hundreds DUSTERS, GOGGLES, AND SCARVES were a must. A duster was a long linen affair which reached nearly to the ankles. My father had a linen cap and goggles—huge things that covered the top half of his face. Ladies wore large hats with heavy veils draped over them, brought down over our ears and fastened in the back. They blew out in the wind as we whizzed along at a thumping fifteen or twenty miles an hour! At the end of the day's run when we removed the goggles we were an odd sight, the lower part of our faces sunburned and windburned and covered with dust, while the goggles had created an owlish effect around the eyes!

One of the delights of summer time when I was a child was to ride in the OPEN trolley car. These were put on about May, I think. The seats were wooden and ran across the width of the trolley. There was a long step that ran the length of the car and to collect the fare the conductor sidled along that step to contact each person. There was a motorman up front who ran the car using as a brake a long handle like a crank which he had to turn furiously to stop the motion of the car. ❧

CHAPTER 3

A BEAUTIFUL NEW HOUSE

When Katharine was nine she was horrified one day to find a FOR SALE sign in front of the house. The real estate agent's name was of course on the sign, and she decided she hated him. "How dare he do such a thing? He almost out-ranked Mr. McGregor in my category of villains!"

She was not consulted, however, and soon became reconciled to the big house on Harvey Street which her father bought.

ೲ It had EVERYTHING. I think there were twenty-one rooms in that house. It sat high up above the street making it necessary to climb quite a few steps to get up to it (also making it hard to drag my bike up and down). Entering the front door from the porch one came into a lovely Dutch hall with a wide stairway of solid natural wood. My father somewhere got a huge moose head which was hung on the landing of the stairs. The beautiful Grandmother's Clock which he gave to my mother stood on the landing, chiming the Whittington chimes. To the left was the library, a big comfortable room with big bookcases and that table that Tom has was in the middle. Facing the front door was my mother's reception room where she received lady callers of an afternoon. It was painted in white enamel and filled with dainty chairs, one of which survives at Betty's. There was also the bane of my existence, TWO WHATNOTS, every shelf of which was full of fragile china and glass "whatnots" or pretty but completely useless things which it was my duty every Saturday morning to DUST.

When a lady would call on Mother, our butler, Alec Harris, black, with a most impressive handle-bar moustache, would open the front door with a flourish, and with great pomp and ceremony usher her into Mother's reception room, receiving on a silver salver her visiting card which he took up to Mother, who after waiting the proper length of time descended the stairs and greeted warmly her guest.

Across the hall and back of the library was the big dining room. Here again Alec was in his element, prancing around the table, whisking things on and off, filling glasses with great dexterity, never spilling a drop. Behind my parents' backs he would look to see if I was watching and then put a full glass of water on his closed fist and, swinging his arm up and down, walk around the table. Not a drop of water ever fell.

There was a butler's pantry back of the dining room and then the big kitchen where Mattie, Alec's plump, cheerful wife held sway. I spent a lot of time with these delightful people. They had a nice bedroom on the third floor with their own bathroom. A laundry adjoined the kitchen and Julie Ruffin, our colored laundress came each week to wash and iron. ૭ৎ

On the second floor were the parents' bedroom, Katharine's adjoining theirs, a guest room with bath, and a sitting room which ran the width of the house at the back. Off this was a screened porch.

The two boys, Frank and Tom, each had a bedroom and den on the third floor, and there was what no home of that era would have been complete without, a "storeroom" where trunks, suitcases, baby coaches, odds and ends of every description collected over the years.

ɞ   I had a small corner there for my doll house and could slip away and do as I pleased with my own things. I was careful to go back downstairs before dark for I was convinced that if I had to be up there in the night a pack of wolves would surely get me!! Where do children get such notions?   ɷ

The answer, of course, is that some of them come from story books and at least one of the more damaging ones directly from parents, as Katharine recalled.

ɞ   I believed very firmly in the arrival of Santa Claus, or "Kris Kingle" as we called him. He was made very real to me each year by my being told to listen for his sleigh bells, and being taken to the front window to look for him. Then I would hear the bells, jingled no doubt by one of my brothers.

"Oh, we must have missed him. I guess he's up on the roof now!" I'd be told, and I'd be hurried to bed to be sure I was ready for him when he came down the chimney. You see, after he had filled the stockings he would actually come into my room to see me—none other, I'm sure, than my brother Tom!

I was around nine years old when I had a traumatic experience. I remember it clearly. I came home from school one day in high dudgeon. "Guess what Eleanor Scattergood told me today?"

"What?"

"She said there was no Kris Kingle!!"

My father, never one to beat around the bush, replied abruptly, "Well, there *isn't*!"

I was appalled. It really shook me. That is one reason I never could bring myself to teach my children about Santa. Another reason was your father's keen sense of honesty, perhaps gleaned partly from his grandfather's (Henry Clay Trumbull's) book, *A Lie Never Justifiable.*

Christmas morning was terribly exciting. My stocking always hung at the foot of my bed. All sorts of delights were in it with something very special in the toe—most likely a lovely little pin or ring or special thing like that.

My grandfather Gillingham always gave me a five-dollar gold piece. I never was very excited about that as it was usually whisked away and put in some mysterious place called a "savings account."

Then we went to see the tree and heaped all around it were beautiful dolls. One year I got a big doll house that my father had made. The furniture in that house was really very special, so much nicer than anything I have seen in later years. I remember the dining room table—it had little leaves so it could be extended. Valerie still has a few remnants of that doll house—the brass bed, some of the dishes and iron pots and pans.

One year I got a gorgeous big doll with real curly brown hair and eyes that opened and closed. Mother had had a complete wardrobe made for her by our dressmaker, Miss Metz. She had kid gloves and little rubber overshoes, silk stockings, a party dress and a two-piece plaid dress, even a fur coat of real sealskin. I'm sorry to say I must have greatly disappointed my mother, but I never cared too much for dolls. I dearly loved my little sets of animals. I had three sizes (I never mixed them, though). The tiny wooden set would be played with one day, and then perhaps the next size. These were very life-like and were made in Germany. The little people to go with this second set were wonderfully and skillfully made. The third set were large enough to be played with in the doll house.

❦

After I was so very sick as a small child the doctor insisted I should wear a "flannel band," a sort of undershirt made of wool. This I had to endure until I was a big girl. A PANTY WAIST in those days had a very different connotation from today. It was part of a little girl's underwear, a cotton contraption worn over her shirt which held an array of buttons. To the pantywaist were fastened my LONG DRAWERS and the white cotton panties with ruffles which were worn over the "longies," and on top of all this TWO flannel petticoats were buttoned. These were all worn until MAY, no matter what the temperature. It was the date that was important, not the weather! It was quite a trick to get my long stockings up over those long drawers.

Mother loved pretty things and she dressed me beautifully. Many of my dresses were hand-embroidered by the nuns at a nearby convent and she would take me with her when she went to pick them up . . . The floors were bare and to the left as we went in was a series of windows with grilles through which we talked with Sister Mary John the Baptist.

One winter Mother bought me a squirrel fur coat. It was soft and gray and warm. With this I wore a large white beaver hat kept on with big pink ribbons tied under my chin. I wore this outfit to church of a Sunday, and on good days we would walk, I skipping ahead of my parents, Mother in long flowing skirts which she had to hold up to keep from sweeping up the pavement. I longed for the day when my skirts would be long enough to hold up. My father, in cutaway coat, gray striped trousers and derby hat could swing his cane with fascinating rhythm.

I have a vivid mental picture of my father and mother getting ready to attend the opera. They had season tickets for the winter and I loved to see them both dressed up for the occasion. They were a handsome couple. I used to wonder how Mother could breathe after Daddy had struggled to get her hooked up down the back in her very tight-fitting princess-style dresses. One dress in particular I loved to see her in—it was red, and she wore those red-beaded slippers that Ginny has now. ᴓ

CHAPTER 4

THE COTTAGE, THE SCHOTTISCHE, THE CHURCH

*T*here were always summer vacations, first at Cape May, New Jersey, from which snapshots survive of the family seated under a canvas on the sand, Katharine in a dark bathing suit with sleeves, a white belt, and pants which reached her knees. Her mother's amounts to a knee-length dress, probably black, with puffed sleeves. She is wearing black stockings and bathing shoes.

There was at least one other vacation, at Swiftwater in the Pocono Mountains of Pennsylvania, before the first summer at Monmouth, Maine, in 1907, when Frank Gillingham rented a cottage on the shore of Lake Cochnewagan, about fifty miles north of Portland.

᪐ In front of that cottage was a pile of rocks where I spent many happy hours with a piece of soap and a cloth, washing them off!! I also had a wooden box covered with a piece of screen in which I had a collection of small frogs and turtles. Once I became concerned about one of them, thinking it must be hungry as it had spurned the flies and other tidbits I had put in for its meals, so I forced the poor thing's mouth open and put a fly inside. The frog died! I was chagrined, but decided they knew best what they wanted to eat. ᪐

In 1909 her father bought two lots and built a cottage further along the lake front. There were a living room with a large stone fireplace, a dining room, a kitchen, six bedrooms (two for the maids) plus attic, and an L-shaped porch, part of which was screened.

✎ Bathroom? There was no such thing. The lake supplied the tub, and pitcher and bowl with "slop bucket" freshened us up in the morning. The outhouse was in back across the road. It had two seats, very cozy and chummy. A box of ashes was kept handy, also some lye.

We had quite a fleet of boats: two Old Town canoes, a Rangeley rowboat, pointed at both ends with a double set of oars and, for fishing comfort, seats with back and arms which could be put on. It was a wonderfully light craft, excelling any other rowboat I ever saw. Then to top it all we had the fastest motorboat on the lake. The exhaust was under water so that we didn't put-put around as most of the other boats did, but just swished quietly by.

I learned to handle a canoe when I was about seven or eight and I never remember upsetting except on purpose when we were swimming.

The Maine Central railroad skirted our lake and roared through Monmouth right back of our cottage . . . The most exciting train was the Bar Harbor Express, bringing summer people from Washington, Philadelphia, and New York. It hardly slowed up going through town, but one day my father had a brainwave . . . He wrote to the president of the railroad asking if they would stop the train at Monmouth on a certain date. Before that we had had to debark at Portland and take a local train. There was great excitement in the town when they knew that the famous train was going to stop to let out the city folks. Everyone who could be there was on hand to see the fun . . . It was a sizable party that descended from the big Pullman cars and the baggage was even more formidable —trunks and trunks and more trunks!

We had a wonderful vegetable garden each summer. My father would take a trip up in May and he and John

Henry Gilman would see that it was well planted . . .
The peas, beans, yellow bantam corn, and potatoes were
the best I've ever eaten—or at least on looking back they
seem very special. I remember our Sunday dinners
especially—we usually had four roast chickens, and my
mother would say that one of them was for Tom. He was
a teen-ager with an inexhaustible appetite. The cook did
twelve new potatoes just for him too.

Every day Helen and I would swim in the lake, rain or
shine. In the afternoons we loved to take one of the
canoes and paddle across the lake where the shore was
lined with trees. We would tie up to a tree, put pillows
and seat backs in the bottom of the canoe, and each curl
up with a good book and a bag of pretzels. Then we might
pull the canoe up on the shore and walk back into the
woods to a beautiful spring where the water was crystal
clear and ice cold. Pretzels make one thirsty, you know.
There was a sandy beach and a little cove nearby and
sometimes we would change into our bathing suits in the
woods and have a swim there. ৶

৺

Back in Philadelphia in wintertime there were dancing
classes, held every Friday at the Manheim Cricket Club.

৶ To get there we had to take a trolley car on Wayne
Avenue and walk what seemed a long distance to the
Club. I carried my dancing pumps in a velvet bag and we
went directly to the dressing room where Mother would
perk up my big satin or taffeta hair ribbons and matching
sash, and I'd change to my pumps.

Mother then joined the other mothers or nurses on one
side of the ballroom and the little girls sat together
opposite them. The little boys were seated at the other
end of our row and at a given signal from the teacher they
would make a mad rush to try to get the girl they wanted
to dance with. They had to halt in front of her and put
their right hand on their stomachs and their left hand
behind them and bow low before her! Needless to say we

were all of a tremor to see who would ask us. There were some boys who were too small or too fat or too clumsy or had freckles or bad breath or some other unfortunate trait and we would try to duck out of their way or pretend we didn't see them if they approached us. Then, of course, there were the goodlooking ones and the good dancers.

I remember two boys, Jack and Bobby Beard, both good dancers and also goodlooking. I loved dancing with them. I think my favorite was Lincoln Gillespie. Link and I loved to do the Schottische together. It was a pretty dance and quite intricate and the teacher singled us out to do it for the others to see, as I recall.

I can't for the life of me remember the name of the teacher, but she was exceedingly graceful and also exceedingly homely. She reminded me of a frog. ❧

❦

When the family moved to Harvey Street it meant a change of schools from All Saints, which Katharine attended when she was six, to the Harvey Street School, and a change of churches, from St. Luke's to St. Peter's.

❧ The rector was a Dr. Keeling. He seemed to me a bit fearsome and grim, though he was probably a very fine man. His curate conducted a confirmation class which I attended. At the age of eleven or twelve it was time for that. I can't remember much about the class, but he did make us learn by heart a lovely collect which I still sometimes use in praying:

"O Lord, forasmuch as without Thee we are not able to please Thee, mercifully grant that Thy Holy Spirit may in all things direct and rule our hearts, through Jesus Christ our Lord. Amen."

Easter was the time for confirmation and I remember the white veil mother had for me to wear. The service was all very impressive, especially as the bishop came to administer the ceremony. I fear I was a very inattentive and UNspiritual candidate. ❧

CHAPTER 5

BRAVE
FOR DADDY
DEAR

*O*ne evening Ida Gillingham
returned with her husband from an evening visiting friends,
feeling very miserable. Within a short time the illness became
serious enough for the doctor to order nursing care.

∽ I have always thought that Mother had pneumonia,
and in those days there were no antibiotics. Things got
worse and I was sent to stay with Aunt Lizzie and Helen,
who then lived quite near to Germantown Friends School
which I was attending. One day for some reason I came
home for something and stopped in to see Mother. I
could sense that she wanted me to stay a while, but a
friend was waiting for me outside so I hurried out to be
with her. I have always had a feeling of real sorrow as I
have remembered this little incident, as it was the last
time I was with my mother until the day she died.

On the morning of December 12, 1911, I was called out
of class and told to go home at once. I realized this must
mean that Mother was either dead or dying. I ran all the
way home, about a mile, I guess it was. As I ran, for
some unaccountable reason, one of the new and very
popular songs of that day kept pace with my feet. It was
"Alexander's Ragtime Band"! What a strange thing! I

have never heard that song since without remembering
that swift flight from school to my home.

Upon arrival I was taken up to her room. Her face was
gray and she could not speak. The rector was there and
the doctor, my brothers and my father and Aunt Lizzie.
The rector served communion and I partook for the first
time. Then I was taken over to give Mother a kiss on her
forehead. It was cold and wet and she looked at me so
sadly. The nurse took me back to the sitting room and
drew me down on the couch and put her arm around me
and we just sat there, saying nothing. What is there to
say? Someone came in in a few minutes—I don't know
who it was—and said, "It's all over." My mother was
forty-seven.

In those days bodies were not whisked off to the
undertakers as they are today . . . The day after she died
her body was still on the bed, and I went into the guest
room where my father had spent the night. He was on his
knees and was CRYING. It is a fearsome thing to see a
strong man cry, and those of you who remember
Grandfather will realize something of my dismay. Once
again I didn't know what to say. He sobbed about going
into their room and seeing her lying there dead. I
remember writing a little verse that I gave to my father:

> Mother's happier now than we can make her here.
> Although we'll long for her and miss
> Her smiling face and loving kiss,
> We'll try to be brave for Daddy dear.

I was twelve years old.

The funeral was held first in our home. Mother's coffin
was placed in her lovely little reception room. It was the
first time I had ever seen a dead person and I could not
really take in what had happened. There was a service at
St. Luke's Church and she was buried under a weeping
willow tree way down in the far corner of the big
graveyard behind the church. In 1940 Grandfather was
buried beside her.

In those days a period of mourning was very carefully

observed and our house had the shades drawn and everything was very quiet. My father would sit in his big black leather chair where I would often climb on his lap and just sit there with him. His head would be in his hand, and every once in a while he would give a big sigh. When I finally returned to school everyone was very kind and considerate to me.

The Harvey Street house had been such a joy to Mother and my father must have sunk a fortune into it, but he couldn't bear to stay there after she died. She had asked Aunt Lizzie to take care of me. This would have separated me from him and so it was decided he would sell the house and we would all move into her house on Greene Street. I think she was very courageous to offer this plan, but my father must have jumped at the idea, for he and my brothers and I all moved into her small house, taking Alec and Mattie with us . . .

Somehow we weathered that year and suddenly we had two weddings. It must have been in November that we went to St. Peter's Church where Frank and Helen Gawthrop were married very quietly, and from the church we proceeded to Dr. Stearns's house where he married my father and Aunt Lizzie!! They and Helen and I returned to the house and as they entered the gate our Irish cook and a chambermaid opened the window and emptied a bag of rice on the newly married couple!! Helen and I were amused but it did not please the newlyweds!!!

The new arrangement pleased me very much as I loved my cousin Helen and at last I had a SISTER!   ⏖

CHAPTER 6

LIGHT
AND
LIFE

ఇం *M*y father's black despair after the death of my mother continued for some months. However, Light and Life were on the way! I have always felt that Mother had a simple faith in Christ. Her last words were, "Jesus Christ who loves me so." Her church life really meant something to her. To my father I believe it had been more or less of a surface religion. It was "the thing to do" to attend the Episcopal church. "Auntie" (Aunt Lizzie) had met a little lady whom she and Mother called Lavvy, who invited her to attend a Bible class in the city taught by Dr. D. M. Stearns. She accepted the invitation and (blessings on Lavvy) her heart was opened to the truths of the Bible in a new way.

After Mother died, Auntie invited my father to go with her to hear these Bible studies. I believe the discovery by my father of my mother's Bible, which he leafed through and found to be all marked up, opened his eyes to a whole new world and made him willing to go with Auntie. Certainly a whole new world opened to him and to me as we began to attend Dr. Stearns's little Reformed Episcopal Church on the corner of Wayne and Chelten Avenues. Bare, cold truths expressed by rote and with great rapidity in the wonderful words of the Nicene Creed and in the ritual of St. Luke's, began to get down into our hearts and to be made realities in our lives. My father's whole attitude was changed and he and I owe to Auntie a debt of gratitude for her courage in bringing us under the teaching of a very wonderful man like dear old Dr. Stearns. It was a new and strange thing to see my father reading his Bible. Being so young, I was easily led along these new paths.

I think it was the second summer after Mother died, that we went to Northfield, Massachusetts. My father did not want to go to Monmouth for the same reason, I suppose, that he didn't want to stay in the Harvey Street house.

There is a lovely big hotel there called the Northfield Inn where we stayed for at least two weeks. Northfield had been the home of the famous evangelist, D. L. Moody, and some of his family were still there. They had an auditorium where very fine speakers gave Bible studies. I remember hearing Dr. G. Campbell Morgan give a talk one day on Psalm 46, contrasting the two titles of God in verses 7 and 11, "The Lord of Hosts," and "the God of Jacob."

Among the guests at the hotel we met and got to know quite well Mr. George C. Stebbins, the hymn-writer. He and his wife and Helen and I used to play cards of an evening together—perhaps it was Five Hundred.

Each evening (or maybe it was just Sunday evening) there was a service for young people on the summit of Round Top, the hill where D. L. Moody and his wife are buried. On his gravestone is the verse, "He that doeth the will of God abideth forever."

I don't remember who spoke one particular night, but I remember being convinced that I needed Christ in my life and so when any such were asked to raise their hands, I put mine up and I remember I was in tears. Helen was aghast and sort of hustled me away and assured me I was all right! I have thought since that this was probably the time when I was converted, though I didn't get any encouragement from Helen. This is the way I remember the incident. I hope I am not misstating it.

Sitting under the simple Bible teaching of old Dr. Stearns (he wasn't a preacher, but a great teacher) opened new vistas to me. Heretofore only my little red prayerbook and hymnal had accompanied me to church. I knew almost nothing about the Bible, but that was all we got from Dr. Stearns. I think I never heard him preach a single message without bringing in the second coming of Christ, which of course was a completely new subject to me.

In this atmosphere I was impressed by the fact that some of the things I had been doing in all innocence were "worldly"! It was worldly to dance, or play cards or go to the theater (there were no movies at that stage in my life). My aunt asked me the question, "If Christ should return would you want to be found doing those things?" "No, I guess not." Finally when I was a junior in high school I gave up dancing (which I dearly loved) and felt I was making progress spiritually. I wish that REAL worldliness had been explained to me! See *The Liberty of Obedience* by E. Elliot!

For a while it seemed to me that a Christian was one who DIDN'T DO a whole list of things. It was a negative approach!

The Church of the Atonement of the Reformed Episcopal denomination was . . . a small chapel-sort of building, seating, I suppose, about two or three hundred people. An ancient organ was played by a dear lady and pumped by hand by a sweating youth whose head appeared regularly from behind the organ as he ground a big handle that supplied air. If he got tired the music might fade out completely!!

The most interesting thing in the church to me was a map of the world up behind the pulpit. It was in two round wooden frames, each containing one of the hemispheres. Behind the map, lights had been installed and little holes made through which these lights shone. Each one represented some mission work in which the church was interested. As I recall there were fifty or sixty lights in all parts of the globe. As a young teen-ager I sat and studied that map Sunday after Sunday and thought of those missionaries so far from home and in such remote places. I supposed that some day I might be going to one such place, but I did hope it would not be Africa!   ๖

CHAPTER 7

SIT STILL, MY DAUGHTER

We used to tease Mother about what a hard life she had at Germantown Friends School—beginning at half past eight, having *two* recesses, and finishing at one o'clock. As for homework, it had apparently not been thought of in those days, or at least at that school. She had no recollection of such a thing.

꿎 Our English teacher was a Mr. Domincovitch. I have often wished I had paid more attention to him. I realize now that he had a great appreciation for good literature and tried to instill some enthusiasm for it into us. He did make me begin to appreciate Grey's Elegy and I read it now with enjoyment . . . How I ever passed chemistry is one of the seven wonders of the world! In the earlier grades we had some real Quakers for teachers —Teacher Helen taught Latin and Teacher Emma English and Teacher Jennie Jones was a whiz at math. Our principal was Master Stanley, a handsome, iron-gray-haired bachelor with a fiery temper. Once he got so angry at someone in the class he picked up a chair and slammed it on the floor and broke it. 꿎

Katharine Gillingham graduated from Germantown Friends in 1917, recipient of the Spoon Girl award, a large ebony-handled silver serving spoon, given to the most out-standing girl in the class. (The Cane Man, the boy who received the silver-headed cane, was Leonard Carmichael who became head of the Smithsonian Institution.) Her father, like many fathers of those days, did not approve of girls going to college, and it never crossed her mind to question his decision.

Later she wondered how she had managed to fill her time after graduation. The United States had entered the Great War only a few weeks before, an event which seemed to have made little difference to the girl, although she occasionally went to roll bandages for the Red Cross. Part of her time was spent in writing letters to soldiers overseas, some of them unknown to her, their names having been given her by the Red Cross as men who had no one to write to them. Others were friends from schooldays, and one of them had been a neighbor during their summers in Monmouth.

∽ Before he left he had taught me a special handshake which just he and I had between us. To me this was very romantic! We wrote regularly and when he returned from France he came to see me. I was really very fond of him and who knows what might have happened if my father had not interfered! He told Dick he did not want him to get serious with me as I was only nineteen. Poor Dick never told me about this, but later I found out from my father what he had done. I can see now that God's hand was in all this, but at the time I was crushed. ∾

Katharine's father presented her with a neat little Buick with a rumble seat, making her one of the first women drivers in Philadelphia. This marvelous new toy not only occupied many an otherwise empty afternoon, but also brought the attentions of a number of envious boys. Some of them, on vacation from college and wearing the uniform of the ROTC, descended on her one day, wanting at least to ride in if not to drive the car. It was not big enough for all of them, so it was agreed that some would take the train into the city while Katharine drove the others. A bet was laid as to which group would get to Broad Street Station first.

ᑌᕼ   I had four of the boys with me and we started down
Lincoln Drive at a terrific speed, probably at least twenty-
five miles per hour. The park guards must have thought I
was doing some war work and had a contingent of
soldiers to get somewhere in a hurry. They just waved us
on and the boys saluted solemnly. The top was back and
the beautiful big fox neckpiece my Daddy had bought me
was flying. We were waiting for the train group when they
emerged from the station.

In a way I was rather lonely that year. Helen had been
married and though I had some good girl friends none of
them was interested in the kind of life I had come to find
satisfying. One day Auntie suggested to me that I might
try praying for a truly Christian friend. This struck me as
an excellent idea and I began. God didn't keep me waiting
very long, for about two weeks later I met a girl I had not
known before although she lived only a block away.
Margaret Haines's brother Charles had been in my class
in the early grades at GFS, but I didn't know his sister.
Knowing Meg opened up a whole new world for me. I
discovered there actually were other young people who
loved the Lord and were very serious in their devotion to
Him—so much so that many of them were aiming at
missionary work on foreign fields. Meg was one of these.
At that time the Student Volunteer Movement was very
active on college campuses and it was a thrill to me to
realize that there was such a wonderful group of young
people with whom I could associate.   ᕼᕔ

In 1920 Meg Haines invited Katharine to attend the Victorious Life Conference in Stony Brook, Long Island. There was a
strong emphasis on foreign missionary work, and toward the
end of the conference the young people were faced with
God's command, "Go into all the world and preach the Gospel."

ᑌᕼ   With fear and trembling I went forward at the call for
volunteers, thereby indicating my willingness to go. As I
considered what a sheltered life I had lived up to that
time, I tried to imagine what it would be like to go to

Africa alone. I was sure it would have to be Africa and I shrank from the idea, quite frankly. However, the Lord was very patient and kind to my fears and gave me a clear verse which has been brought back to me repeatedly during my life—Naomi's word to her daughter-in-law Ruth, "Sit still, my daughter, until thou know how the matter will fall."

And what a surprise He had for me as I waited to see how the matter would fall! ∾

Later that summer Meg Haines invited Katharine to a house party at her summer home in Castine, Maine.

∾ I took the train from Monmouth to Portland and then another train from Portland to Rockland on Penobscot Bay. There I boarded a boat that plied to various places on the Bay. A thick fog enveloped us before we had gone very far. The Bay was dotted with juttings of rock and islands of various sizes and I wondered how the captain would negotiate them all. I soon found out. The foghorn would blast every few seconds. If there was a faint echo from some direction he knew which island it was and would steer accordingly.

As we drew in to the dock at Castine I saw the smiling faces of Meg and my two friends Winnie and Betty. Towering behind them was a figure I was to come to know and love, the only man in the party, Phil Howard! ∾

CHAPTER 8

A
MAN OF
DECISION

A year and a half before young Tom Gillingham found that the "surprise" was not a bicycle but a baby sister, a young couple in St. Marks Square in West Philadelphia celebrated the birth of their firstborn. They were Philip Eugene Howard, son of Eugene Howard, a physician from Massachusetts, and Philip's wife, Annie Slosson Trumbull Howard, daughter of Henry Clay Trumbull, a Civil War chaplain and later editor of *The Sunday School Times*. Their son Philip, Jr., was born in January of 1898.

When he was about three years old he demonstrated a sort of clairvoyance which startled his parents on several later occasions. While playing with his toys one day he suddenly looked up and said, "Mother, the house is going to burn down today." It was a big house in Haverford, Pennsylvania, and it burned to the ground that afternoon. The question is naturally raised as to whether the little boy had something to do with it, but the fire was found to have started in a faulty flue.

His mother, like most middle-class housewives at that time, had one maid who seemed to do almost everything. Her (his mother's) diary records many headaches and mornings in bed; train trips into Philadelphia for lunch at Wanamaker's Tea Room alone or with friends; an occasional afternoon of baking "chocolate jumbles" or sorting things in the storeroom. She began at a young age to be plagued by arthritis which slowly crippled her, but she continued to manage lunches out, dinners at friends' homes, evening lectures and concerts, and usually church on Sundays.

Her husband, Philip, who worked with his father-in-law at "the S.S.T.," took his two sons, Philip, Jr., and "Trum" to Rome for a Sunday School Convention in 1907. Bored in the hotel one day the boys went out onto a balcony and began firing small stones at the wine bottles a merchant had set out for sale on the street. To their amazement Philip's stone hit its target, the wine ran over the sidewalk, the merchant shouted and waved his arms, looking for the culprits who had ducked out of sight. Philip had a tender conscience, confessed what he had done, and his father made him pay for the damage.

The boy remembered his father as "a patient, cheerful, optimistic man," whose powers of concentration were notable: his study was the landing of the stairs. There he would sit and write, with all the family traffic coming and going. He was always available to his four children (two girls, Alice and Anne, were born in 1902 and 1909), not minding their interruptions, and interested in all that interested them.

During the summer when Philip was thirteen he went with the family, as Katharine Gillingham did one year later, to D. L. Moody's conference grounds at Northfield, Massachusetts. His father had forbidden him to have firecrackers for July Fourth. Too dangerous, he said. Philip decided he could take care of himself. He managed to get hold of some dynamite caps, sneaked out of the house before dawn, and went with a friend to a nearby farm where he asked the farmer to help him fire off the caps. They put them on the ground, lit the fuse, and ran to a safe distance. Nothing happened. Impatient, all three closed in, the farmer kicked the pile, the caps exploded, and a tiny piece of copper pierced Philip's left eye. The doctor recommended that he be taken at once to a hospital in Philadelphia, an overnight train trip on which his father accompanied him. The train had to make unscheduled stops for ice in order to keep a cold pack on the eye. The doctor who operated on him said that if there had been no ice available, or if they had arrived one hour later, Philip would have lost both eyes instead of only one. It was a tough lesson in the rewards of disobedience, one which his children later heard often reviewed.

Pneumonia brought Philip very near to death when he was seventeen years old. For months he lay sick—the only months when there is more than passing mention of him in his mother's diary ("Dear Philip is worse," "Had the doctor for dear Philip"). When the doctor prescribed brandy the boy, determined never to allow a drop of alcohol to pass his lips (a vow he kept for life), refused to take even the smallest sip. God honored the boy's promise, heard the prayers of his parents, and healed him.

To his small cousin, Gurdon Scoville, Philip

represented all that a strong big brother means. I watched him one day with admiration climb up the high steep roof to a weathervane of our neighbor's house—whether out of daring or for a purpose I don't know. Another day I was too tired to push my bicycle up the steep hill to reach home. He found me sitting disconsolate in the road, picked up the bicycle on his shoulder and led me up the hill.

Philip shared his father's love for wildlife and the outdoors, revelling in the surroundings of the family's summer home in Franconia, New Hampshire, where he canoed, fished, hiked, climbed the White Mountains (at least once in the company of poet Robert Frost who lived nearby), and continued his own study of birds, begun in the woods near Swarthmore, Pennsylvania, where they lived. Long before "bird-watching" was heard of, young Philip was spending whole days alone in the forests, standing quietly with hands behind him (as he taught his own children to do years later), observing the little creatures, then recording his observations, making lists of species seen, and imitating their calls with such perfection that he was able to fool the experts of the Delaware Valley Ornithological Club of which he became a member. He would occasionally hide in the bushes and give the call of a rare bird, or one that was not usually seen in that region, to the great bafflement and excitement of fellow club members—until they found that the source was human.

A conscientious but not very imaginative diary-keeper for

four years (1916 through 1919), he recorded his rising and retiring times (usually before six A.M. and anywhere from nine to midnight), the number of miles hiked (ten miles were not unusual; fifteen and more occasionally), books read, birds seen, chores done. A sample:

> Friday, June 9, 1916. Rose 6:30. Read paper. After breakfast came up to Philadelphia. Stopped at father's office to get advice as to shirts, went out to buy some and did *not* buy any. After lunch unpacked suitcase, straightened room and downstairs; took pants to tailor's; pressed suit; got a collar box from Mrs. Hulbert; wrote to her and Aunt Irene; fixed accounts and records. Class banquet. Took C. home. Stayed awhile. Talked with Aunt Sophy. Bed 12:00 (last bed at 12:00—May 5).

"C." was Charlotte Bunting, a name we often heard when our parents talked of "old flames." No one but Charlotte had ever caught Philip Howard's eye, so far as we knew then, while Mother had quite a list of boyfriends.

"Caught 'singing toad'," he writes one day, and on another, "Found den of six large snakes. One struck at me and his mouth showed white." On August 1, at a boys' camp in Pennsylvania, "Bird-tree-flower walk. Swim. Got a dandy letter from C. 12 pages. A book from father. A letter from mother."

There is very little indication of spiritual interest until August 2, 1916, when he attended two meetings at Collegeville, Pennsylvania. He makes no mention of the speakers, but writes, "Had a wonderful talk with Uncle Charley and now I am happy, happy, happy. I feel a wonderful peace. Everything seems all right. Thank the Lord."

Several years later in a vesper talk at a summer conference he described what happened that day:

> Like many of you, I was brought up in a Christian home, came to Christ at an early age, struggled along, falling, and getting up again. But finally I saw the truth in II Corinthians 12:9, "My grace is sufficient for thee." I laid the whole thing at Jesus' feet, even my faith and trust, and He gave me faith to believe that His grace was sufficient for me.

The next day's diary entry begins,

Rose 6:00, read Bible. Sunrise meeting. Bible hour under Dr. Crowell. He is straight on everything. Sermon by Dr. C. Armand Miller. Long talk and prayer with Uncle Charley. Everything is all right now. I broke down under the weight of my own thoughts and Christ came in. Later I was homesick and through prayer that entirely left me. Walk with Uncle C. Sunset meeting. Evening meeting. Short talk with Uncle C. Bed 9:45.

The vesper talk continues:

The day after my new decision as I was talking with a very dear friend about it, having had no emotion whatever, two things came over me just like waves of the ocean,—the fact of my own foolishness and worthlessness in trying to fight it out in my own strength, even with Christ's help, and the fact that Christ's grace was infinitely more than sufficient. What joy I felt in the fact that Christ was my victory and strength and life.

In his diary on August 4 he wrote,

Had morning watch [private devotions]. Today attended sunrise meeting, Bible hour, conference, sunset, and evening meetings. Had sand tennis in p.m. with the Isenberg girls . . . Wrote up my wonderful experience. Had talk with Dr. Crowell after meeting. He's great. Then had a friendly talk with Uncle C. Prayer with both in p.m. Bed 11:15.

August 6. Rose 6:10. Short morning watch. After sunrise meeting, Christ led the first soul through me to Himself that has ever been led through me. Praise God!

He later looked on this spiritual awakening as the Lord's preparing him for the testings of college life, where he would encounter Modernism and Higher Criticism, taught by people who

stripped God's Word of everything it meant to me—I never saw anything like it. But God gave me grace to get up early in the morning and listen to him speak through his Word, and talk to him in prayer, and Christ was giving me victory all through each day. There was one senior with whom I had fellowship, and we would slip into a classroom at night for prayer, the best times I ever had. Towards the end of the year we got a prayer group together.

An incident that must have taken place shortly after this was what his cousin Gurdon Scoville called his most important memory of Phil:

He was eighteen, a freshman at Haverford College, and I was twelve. One afternoon in his room he talked to me about receiving Jesus Christ as my Savior and entering into a lifetime covenant to read His Word daily and carry it with me wherever I went. That afternoon God used Phil to lead me into a covenant relation with my Lord which has been sustained through the years, not only in the daily reading and carrying of the Word but in entering into a new life in Christ that still keeps unfolding in new and more glorious ways forty-five years later.

In 1915 his father had inscribed his book, *Their Call to Service*, "To Philip E. Howard Jr., with the love of his father, who prays that the call to service may be heard and heeded by him at all times." Philip's being one-eyed barred him from military service in World War I, but having heard God's definite call to Christian service he accepted an invitation from Mr. George T. B. Davis, director of the Pocket Testament League, to travel with him in army camps as a sort of apprentice/assistant.

The diary records train journeys as far south as the Mexican border, staying in hotels or living in the barracks, taking dictation from Mr. Davis by hand for hours at a stretch, holding meetings, distributing free New Testaments, playing the piano for the men, witnessing in quiet conversations with individuals. Frequent entries reveal the careful self-discipline of rising early enough to read the Bible, taking long walks for exercise, struggling weekly with accounts, writing dutifully to parents, cousins, aunts, reading edifying books. In Tucson he actually went to a Sam Fairbanks "movie show" with George —"great show, clean, fine. Good French war pictures, educational, and animated cartoons. Back to the Y. Walk. Eats. Bed 11:00."

In the first four months the two men distributed fourteen thousand pocket-size New Testaments, and thirty-five hundred men said they would take Christ as Savior.

On Sunday, April 14, 1918, at a missionary conference in Nyack, New York, the diary notes, "God led four men to Christ through me, praise Him! Fine talk with a woman African missionary." That much is in pencil. Inked in at the bottom of the page: "Missionary decision." No other comment, but he filled in details of his missionary call in his vesper talk:

> The appeal kept coming and coming to me, and every time I came to a missionary verse in my Bible reading, it hit me like a stone. Finally one morning I heard a fellow singing. It wasn't the hymn that brought me to it, it was Christ himself. The song was "Beneath the Cross of Jesus." I was thinking there was so much to give up, I loved my home, and luxuries, but I thank God that he finally gave me the power to make the decision. One phrase helped me, "I ask no other sunshine than the sunshine of his face." When I thought of that, I couldn't stand it any longer, and said, "Lord, here is my decision to go as a foreign missionary."

He continued his work with Mr. Davis. At Camp Merritt:

> I went up to one fellow and asked, "Would you like a Testament?" His face brightened up as he said, in a Southern voice, "Oh yes, suh, I'd like one." He said it in such a way that I wondered at the tone. Then I thought of something that might be hindering. "Can you read?" I asked. "No," he replied, with a quiet smile. "I've been trying to learn for a long time, but I can't do much. But I'm awful glad for what I do know."
>
> He seemed so interested that I said, "Suppose you take one and try to get someone to read it to you each day." "I'll certainly do all I can with it," he said. So I signed a card for him, and he took the Testament. Then I spoke to him about Christ. He spoke out then in such a way that I knew the Lord was working. "Come over by this coal box," I said, "away from the crowd." He followed, and then he told me something like this:
>
> "I never made a decision for Christ, but I want to. God has been dealing with me a long while. For the last three weeks I've been seeking after the Lord and praying to him every night. I saw a fellow make the decision at the 'Y' the other

night. But I can't get away from the old cussin'—I gave up drinkin'. Many a time I've been in jail because of drink, and I know that if a fellow goes across the pond, and gets killed, if he isn't saved he's going straight to hell. But if he is saved, it's all right. Many a preacher has been after me for ten years. But always there's something holdin' me back."

As he talked he broke down and pulled out his handkerchief. Then I talked as I very seldom find myself talking. The Lord gave me many verses to use. I told the fellow a little of my own experience. Finally he said, with his voice trembling, "I'll take him," and gripped my hand hard. Then I said, "Will you write that here in the corner?" I had forgotten he could not write. He said, his voice still trembling, "You write and I'll touch the pencil." So as I wrote "I accept Christ," he laid a firm, warm hand on mine. Then he gripped my hands again, and thanked me for coming down.

In July of that year Philip attended a Victorious Life Conference at Princeton as Katharine Gillingham was to do two years later at Stony Brook.

The end of the Great War is passed over with a laconic note in his diary on Sunday the twenty-first: "Great American victory announced by firebells and chimes." More momentous to him was what took place at the conference a few days later. An invitation was given for all missionary volunteers to go to the platform. Philip went, of course, along with his friend Donald Grey Barnhouse with whom he was later to work in Belgium, Robert McQuilkin, later the founder of Columbia Bible College, and Margaret Haines, who was to go to India as a missionary and then to have an important part in the establishment of the Inter-Varsity Christian Fellowship in America. The volunteers sang together "Where He Leads Me I Will Follow" and "O Zion, Haste."

A lifetime decision had been made: Philip Howard would do anything God wanted him to do. But then came the perplexing question: What, exactly, did God want of him now? Two immediate options were before him: continue with the Pocket Testament League or go to college. "Much puzzled. Can't sleep." He chose to stay with the League for the rest of that year.

Margaret Haines's name begins to occur more frequently in

the diary. Her mother often invited Philip to meals. He went to their summer home in Castine, Maine, for two weeks. Mrs. Haines sent him a picture of Margaret when he got home. Then one day in November (the army camps in which he was working were within easy distance of Philadelphia) he wrote, "Ride with Katharine Gillingham and Margaret in Katharine Gillingham's Buick roadster . . . Wonderful day." A week later he recorded another walk with Margaret, and in late December, while Mrs. Haines was reading aloud to her guests following a Sunday lunch his attention was distracted— "Katharine Gillingham came in." On January 3, 1919, he decided it was time to burn Charlotte's letters. On rereading them, however, he decided against it, and telephoned her instead. She was "very cordial and pleasant." The next day it was dinner again at the Haineses' with a group that included Katharine.

The young man must have spoken to his family of Margaret's friend. His mother no doubt judged his interest to be more than routine and invited Margaret, Katharine, and two of Philip's men friends to a birthday party. In March he went to the Gillingham home for dinner. September brought another invitation to the Haineses' summer home in Maine where his decision to be a missionary was confirmed as he conversed with other houseguests—a missionary from Africa and a couple with whom he would later work, Ralph and Edith Norton, founders of the Belgian Gospel Mission.

October 18, 1919—"To K's for supper."

November 27—"Took M. to Penn-Cornell game."

November 29—"Supper at KG's."

December 17—"Philadelphia Orchestra with Alice Adams."

December 22—"To C's" (Charlotte's).

The diaries end with 1919, not having revealed any special preference for one of the girls above another.

In September of 1920 Mrs Haines once more invited the young man to her home—her beautiful summer home this time, in Castine, Maine, along with other friends of Margaret's, for what was then called a house party. It was another opportunity to bring her daughter and this fine young prospect together.

It is not certain that Phil knew who the other guests were to be. Perhaps, in accepting the invitation, he was thinking of it as an opportunity to sort out the possibilities in the group of very nice young women (Charlotte and Alice would certainly not be among them, however), or perhaps it was simply the prospect of a pleasant weekend in a wonderful place, but standing with Margaret on the Haineses' private dock as one of her guests stepped off the boat, he suddenly knew his preference.

CHAPTER 9

A
CHRISTIAN HOME
IS BORN

*I*t was a Thursday when Katharine arrived in Castine. Mrs. Haines placed her next to Phil Howard at the table.

ୡ An occasional quick glance at his face made me like him very much, but I was quite sure he was Meg's special friend so gave him only the most casual and friendly thoughts . . . We had some lovely drives and picnics during the next couple of days, we four girls and Phil. I remember once as she was tearing along the road (Meg was a regular Jehu when it came to driving) she suddenly burst into a sort of song: "Oh, it's great to be FREE!" We all laughed, thinking she really wasn't that way at all, but almost committed to Phil.

Early Sunday morning Phil came to me with a special request. Could we take a walk after dinner? I thought the "we" referred to all of us and so told the rest of the party that Phil wanted to take a walk that afternoon. We ALL did! After supper as we were getting ready to attend the village church he came to me and asked if I would walk to church with him. I thought it was sort of funny that he was so crazy to walk again after the long walk we all had had that day, but I consented and we started off. We had not gone far, however, before the car with the rest of the party pulled up beside us and urged us to get in. I was not sorry.

At the end of the church service Phil once again asked me to walk home with him. Actually he was getting desperate as he was leaving the next day to return to Franconia [New Hampshire, where his family had their summer home].

Nothing interfered this time with the walk. ⮞

A quiet Sunday evening in the little coastal town, a fresh salt breeze moving the stately elms, and a slender, pretty, laughing girl (*what* was this walk all about?) by the side of the thin, thoughtful, long-legged man eight inches taller (will such a lady have such as I—a man with only one eye?).

⮜ He wasted no time at all in what he wanted to say to me. He loved me and would I marry him?

It may sound strange for me to say that I was completely unprepared for this, thinking as I did that he and Meg were eventually to link up. It was literally a case of, "Oh, this is *so* sudden!"

He pleaded his case earnestly, but all I could say then was that I could not give him an answer one way or the other. ⮞

Phil was a senior at the University of Pennsylvania that year, living with his family in Swarthmore, traveling as often as possible the twelve or fifteen miles by trolley car to the Gillingham home in Germantown, hoping each time for an answer to his question. After six weeks patience had had "her perfect work," and in mid-October she said Yes.

⮜ He hurried upstairs to our sitting room where he found my father and told him he wanted to marry his daughter. My father was less than enthusiastic and the best he could say for his future son-in-law was a grudging, "Well, at least you're a Christian." ⮞

Frank Gillingham, a hardheaded businessman, had in mind for Katharine something quite other than Philip Howard, the quiet student from a different social set. A Christian, yes, but perhaps carrying that aspect of things a bit farther than necessary.

In November Philip gave his fiancée a small leather-bound Bible inscribed "To dearest Kath with my best love and great joy and thankfulness for our love in Christ, from her own Phil." He added the reference, Phil. 1:3, "I thank my God upon every remembrance of you." Underneath his inscription Katharine wrote, "Dear Lord Jesus, bless Phil and keep him always in Thy will. Oh, make me worthy of him and fit us both for the place Thou hast for us. I thank Thee, Lord Jesus, for Thyself, and I pray Thee to make Thyself more and more real to me every day." At the bottom of the page she noted, "Our verse—Ps. 71:16" ("I will go in the strength of the Lord GOD: I will make mention of thy righteousness, even of thine only").

Philip Howard earned a Phi Beta Kappa key and graduated from the university in June of 1921. In his commencement address at Wheaton College in Illinois in 1947 he said,

> It is twenty-six years since I sat with a large company of students on Commencement Day, waiting to receive diplomas, as you are now waiting for yours, and I can recall something of the mingled feelings that I had on that day—joy over the completion of the course, and a good deal of apprehension as I looked into the future, wondering whether I should be able to build well. In all these years I have sought to serve God, and I want to join a multitude of others who have done likewise, in bearing testimony to His boundless love and mercy, and to say from a full heart that His grace is sufficient for every need, and that there is no service so joyous and satisfying as His.

A man did not think of taking unto himself a wife in those days until he had some idea of how he would support her. Phil had no money, so he took a job as physical education instructor and study hall supervisor at Haverford Boys' School while attending the Bible Institute of Pennsylvania with his fiancée. They were one in their desire to be missionaries, and prayed together during this year for God's direction as to where to go. Because the work of the Belgian Gospel

Mission seemed to come to their attention repeatedly, from different sources, they took this as the answer.

Twenty-one months after the proposal in Maine they were married. The wedding on June 14, 1922, in the little chapel of the Church of the Atonement, was simple and quiet. The Wedding Breakfast at home for the immediate families proved to be less simple and considerably less quiet, Phil's "immediate" family comprising innumerable aunts, uncles, and cousins. The honeymoon began with a train trip to New York, then a boat to Fall River, Massachusetts, a night in Boston and another train to Littleton, New Hampshire. By carriage they reached at last Gale Cottage, a charming sort of old lodge built by a great-uncle of Phil's in Franconia.

ᴄ᾿ᴐ I'm sure we must have had something besides ham to eat during those two weeks, but I can't remember anything due to the fact that in my ignorance I bought A HAM for the two of us! My knowledge of cooking was practically NIL at that time. At home we had always had maids and I suppose it never occurred to me that I would ever have to do much cooking. Well, Phil [who did know how to make oatmeal and coffee, he told his children years later] was a saint about the meals I prepared—never do I remember his complaining about them, and I had to learn the hard way. Blessings on whoever it was who gave us a Fanny Farmer cookbook for a wedding present! ᴄ᾿ᴐ

A brief note carries perhaps far more weight than the couple realized at the time. It gives the key to the establishment of a Christian marriage and a Christian home:

ᴄ᾿ᴐ It was shortly after we were married that we decided to have special prayer together every Saturday night, spreading before God our needs, those of our children, and giving thanks for all His benefits. ᴄ᾿ᴐ

CHAPTER 10

THE NEW MISSIONARIES

⌒ *T*he missionary candidate of today faces a formidable screening process, along with training in linguistics, anthropology, cultures, etc. etc. He must live and operate under the watchful eyes of seasoned and experienced supervisors and be questioned by members of the mission board. He must have had a certain amount of Bible training and experience in Christian work at home. This is all good, no doubt, and should help to eliminate those who are not qualified for missionary work.

Neither Phil nor I had any of the above preparation when we were accepted by the Belgian Gospel Mission. I should correct that statement. Phil HAD had experience in personal work in the army camps and at Camp Allagash. He also had had some classes in Bible, as I had had, but other than that we were surely a couple of babes in the woods when we sailed for Belgium in the middle of July, 1922. ⌒

The Nortons and Philip's parents accompanied them on the S.S. *Lapland* of the Red Star Line, his father having been asked to write a book on the mission's history, *A New Invasion of Belgium*.

An old veteran missionary sent a letter to Philip and Katharine on the steamer, wishing them a happy and helpful time, and adding suggestions to make it so.

> See all you can, on board ship, everywhere. If conditions will permit of it, make the acquaintance of the Chief Engineer, and see the "works" of the boat! They are worth seeing!! Never join the ranks of those who think sanctification means shutting your eyes to everything!! . . .
>
> God's way of speaking to you and of getting at you will be through His Word. Dwell in it, therefore. Begin each day with a portion of it. Pray for grace to see when He is speaking to you, and for grace to adjust yourself to what He thus shows you. Do that and you will be a successful Christian and missionary wherever you are.
>
> If it has not already been done, somewhere in the mid-Atlantic just dump overboard all the supposed superiority we Americans think we have over most other folks! Enter Belgium merely as a sinner-saved-by-grace, and not as an American! . . . Don't be going around with a chip on your shoulder looking for your rights. I do not say this because I have seen anything in you which leads me to think it necessary, for, so far as I have observed, you are free from it all. I do know human nature a bit, though, and you will need to keep close to the Lord to prevent this sort of thing coming into your life.
>
> Mr. Hoste [director of the China Inland Mission] once said to me, as I was about to take up a new responsibility, "Mr. Whittlesey, you may expect all the honor and esteem you are worthy of receiving, and no more!" A good text: "Let your yieldingness be known unto all men" Phil. 4:5, margin.

It was a perfect crossing with a warm west wind all the way, and the newlyweds proved to be "good sailors." After a month in a pension they found an apartment,

ᑌᕼ up fifty-eight steps on the third floor of a tall dingy building over a wineshop, run by a jittery little English woman who had married a Belgian. The apartment was furnished with huge and hideous pieces of miscellaneous furniture. There was no running water and Phil had to lug it up from a half-flight down where we had a sort of bathroom. The bathing problem loomed large on our horizon! A few inches of tepid water in a basin is certainly better than nothing, but a good hot bath means much to an American used to as many as one wishes every week. Mr. and Mrs. Norton very kindly invited us to avail ourselves of the luxury of their bathtub, so every Saturday afternoon we packed a suitcase with our towels, soap, and clean clothing and hopped a tram to go and have a hot bath.

My father was horrified that we had no water in our apartment and sent us money to have it piped up. This was a great boon and we had a sink put in the kitchen where we washed not only our dishes but ourselves.

One coal stove in the living room heated the three rooms and again meant more lugging, this time from the cellar. Up the fifty-eight-plus steps with the coal, down again with the ashes. Our windows looked out on a grimy collection of chimneypots. Phil bought me a dear little canary who sang most cheerfully and was a real joy to me.

Altogether, as I look back on that first home, it was pretty bleak, but we were not aware of this, being very much in love and happy just to have a little place all our own.

French lessons began in earnest soon after we arrived, with M. Boutee, a Frenchman who had an excellent accent and teeth always filled with food which had a way of landing on the table in front of us as he tried to enunciate his words clearly for our benefit!   ๛

It was a shock one day when the Nortons informed Phil that he was immediately to take over the children's work in the slums of Brussels.

๛ It is hard enough for a foreigner with school and college French to stumble along when one's ear is not attuned to the language. To understand CHILDREN is by far the most difficult of all . . . Thursday afternoons came around all too quickly and often. As the weather got colder and damper and rainier, which was the usual kind of weather from about November to June, these children would arrive wearing black aprons (even the little boys) and big black mufflers around their necks. Usually they wore no panties under the aprons, so their little rears and legs would be purple with cold, but if their necks were warm that seemed to suffice! ❧

The Howards' closest friends were a young couple whom they had met at the Stony Brook Conference just before they left America—John and Grace Winston. Early in 1923 Katharine felt a bit jealous when Grace whispered to her that she was to have a baby ("the word pregnant was not used in polite circles"). Only a short time later Katharine found herself in the same wonderful condition.

❧ The idea of trudging up and down fifty-eight steps with a baby and hauling a folding baby coach at the same time presented problems so we decided it was time to look for another place to live. ❧

They found a cheerful three-room apartment at 52 Rue Ernest Laude. They had a bathtub installed in the kitchen with a *chauffe-bain,* a coil water heater.

Philip Gillingham Howard was born on December 9, 1923, "a joy and delight," but Katharine felt she was "a very poor specimen of a missionary" then, being so taken up with the care of the child. One day she was asked to teach the Bible to a group of women—in French, of course.

❧ I tried to wriggle out of it but Philippians 4:13 kept recurring to me ("I can do all things through Christ who strengthens me"), until I finally had to say I'd try to do it. I have since wondered what the ladies got out of my feeble efforts, but I know the experience was good for me. ❧

❧

A test of trust in God from which few Christians are exempt is that of money. It is a rare missionary who is not sorely tested in this matter.

The Howards received a salary of one hundred dollars per month. One day they received

ൟ   a financial blow—the Belgian government informed us that we must pay a fifty dollar income tax for the year of 1923. You can imagine what it meant to cut our month's salary in half, but somehow we managed to scrape it together and pay it. The next month came another notice saying we had to pay one hundred dollars for the year 1924. I don't remember how we managed this but we did. The final blow came in May. A third notice for our tax of 1925, two hundred dollars.

Just at that time Dad [remember the autobiography was written for us children, so she calls him Dad] had to go to Switzerland for mission business and there I sat, wondering and praying about this latest crack at our already slim bank balance. While he was away I received a cable from his father, "Draw on your account to the extent of $200."

I do not think we had mentioned our problem to our families in the U.S. The cable ended, "Letter follows." I immediately sent this good news on to Dad. When Grandpa's letter came he told us that he had been in New York and had stopped to see an old lady who had been a friend of *The Sunday School Times* for many years. Just as he was leaving she said, "By the way, you have a son with the Belgian Gospel Mission, haven't you?" She handed him a check for two hundred dollars for us. We had never heard of her and never heard from her again! Philippians 4:19!!   ൟ

The Word of God was always the reference point for the Howard family. If God had something to say on any matter, they listened. Philip's exquisitely sensitive conscience made him frugal almost to a fault, since he regarded all that came into his hands as the Lord's money. "Need" was carefully distinguished from "want," and the words of the passage referred to above governed their thinking: "My God shall supply all your need according to his riches in glory by Christ Jesus" (AV).

CHAPTER 11

HE LIVED
WHAT HE
TAUGHT US

*F*ive years of missionary work had passed, and 1927 was the year of furlough for the Howards. As Charles Lindbergh was winging his way east across the Atlantic in the fragile *Spirit of St. Louis* they were sailing west with their two children, Philip who was now three, and Elisabeth, five months. While Katharine visited her father and stepmother on a farm in Pennsylvania, Philip went at the urgent invitation of his uncle Charley to Castine, Maine, taking little Philip with him. He had a fairly good idea what Uncle Charley had in mind, having received a letter from him in Belgium asking him seriously to consider joining *The Sunday School Times* as associate editor. This request had been prayed over and turned down, as they were then "so busy and deep in the work of the Mission that we could not imagine leaving it," Katharine wrote, remembering also that her husband had said that one thing he would certainly *never* do was work for the S.S.T.

ᑫ Uncle Charley put up strong reasons why he needed his nephew with him. Dad returned to the farm and we struggled with this proposition, neither one of us wanted even to consider it, and we fought against the idea for a while, though all the time feeling that this was what God wanted us to do. It was the hardest decision we had ever had to make. ❧

As I read Mother's story, I saw in that decision a revelation of the vital principles of my parents' lives: they loved God, they trusted Him, they meant to obey Him no matter what the sacrifice, no matter how their obedience might change the course of their lives.

❧ There was another baby on the way. I could not imagine having any other doctor than the brilliant Belgian, Dr. Cheval. Everything in our new house in Brussels was so shiny and attractive and a perfect home, with a full bathroom, a dear little walled-in garden, wide open spaces for the children to play in—oh, I was very unhappy about not going back there!

We stayed, and I fear our first year was lived NOT TRIUMPHANTLY BUT SOMEHOW! We had to hurry to buy a house and it had to be CHEAP. IT WAS! ❧

❦

My own memories of 103 West Washington Lane in Germantown begin, I suppose, when I was three or four years old. It was a double house, like the one Mother was born in. There were a small bank of grass between us and the sidewalk, a narrow side yard, and a back yard big enough for a sandbox, a clothesline, and a little strip of flower garden.

We had a tiled vestibule, a dark front hall with stairs running up the right side, a living room with mantel but no fireplace, a dining room with a bay window that looked straight into the bay window of the house next door, a pantry, a kitchen, and what we called the shed, a sort of lean-to at the back which held washtubs and tools. Upstairs were three bedrooms and one bathroom, on the third floor two more bedrooms and a storeroom. To me it was a perfectly good house, and it was not until years later that I realized how gloomy and cramped it was to my parents, used as they were to much more spacious homes. If we had heard them complain we would have felt deprived, for children are quick to pick up the parents' attitudes to everything. Because they never betrayed a hint of discontent that I recall we took the house for granted, as we did also the oriental rugs, beautiful pieces of antique furniture, and the sterling silver which my mother had from her family. Not until I reached my teens did I notice that not everyone walked on oriental rugs or ate with sterling silver every day.

ᚒ

That was the house we lived in. What was happening there was something far greater than its walls and its furniture and pictures and books. A home was being established. Its foundation was love for God, trust in His providence, obedience to His Word. God was there, talked about, talked to, *present*.

"The children of your servants will live in your presence; their descendants will be established before you" (Ps. 102:28 NIV).

When I was a child I knew almost nothing of evil. T. S. Eliot wrote, "If humility and purity be not in the heart, they are not in the home; and if they are not in the home, they are not in the City." Was our home not a place of humility and purity? I think it was. It was also a place of peace. We never heard our parents raise their voices to each other, and very seldom to us. If we wanted someone in another room or on another floor we did not shout, we went where they were.

Our parents did not, as a rule, slam doors or thunder up and down the stairs and did not expect us to. Lest any reader feel, however, that they set an unattainable example, let me say that there were exceptions. My father inherited the famous temper of one of his grandfathers. There were a few occasions when he did slam doors, thunder up the stairs, or leap so furiously from the table as to throw his chair over backwards. Because these *were* exceptions we children were stunned to silence, and his humble apologies later reinforced the standard. He was greatly ashamed of his failures and prayed for victory over them. Over the years we saw his prayers answered, and at a recent family reunion the younger three of our family said they had seldom witnessed the scenes we older ones remembered so well.

It is amazing how often children do what is expected of them when the example is consistently set by both father and mother. My stepdaughter Katherine Scamman, the lovely mother of four who now live in Scotland, has a very soft voice. When my husband and I visit them we notice that the children, some of whom are in their teens, speak softly. We also notice that parents who habitually scream at their children have children who scream.

The example of parents, for good or ill, is an influence far more profound than can be measured. Their discipline and orderliness, their calm control were not things we noticed at all as children, of course. It was just the way things were at home, and hence the way we thought things were supposed to be, so we were horribly shocked when we visited homes where things were not disciplined, orderly, and calm. As I look back I know that it was the presence of God that made the difference. Over the front door bell button hung a little copper plate with these words:

> Christ is the Head of this house,
> The unseen Guest at every meal,
> The silent Listener to every conversation.

To a thoughtful child those words create an aura.

Our parents understood very clearly that the principles they taught their children would have meager effect if they were not strongly fortified by the pattern of their own lives. "To give children good instruction and a bad example," wrote Archbishop Tillotson, "is but beckoning to them with the head to show them the way to heaven while we take them by the hand and lead them in the way to hell" (J. C. Ryle, *The Duties of Parents*).

The latter part of the century in which I have lived bears a notable resemblance to what St. Paul called "the last days," by which I assume he meant the times in which the young Timothy would live, nearly two thousand years ago:

> You must realise that in the last days the times will be full of danger. Men will become utterly self-centred, greedy for money, full of big words. They will be proud and abusive,

without any regard for what their parents taught them. They will be utterly lacking in gratitude, reverence and normal human affections. They will be remorseless, scandal-mongers, uncontrolled and violent and haters of all that is good. They will be treacherous, reckless and arrogant, loving what gives them pleasure instead of loving God. They will maintain a façade of "religion" but their life denies its truth (2 Tim. 3:1–7 PHILLIPS).

It appears that men like my father were a rare breed even back in Timothy's time. They still are. Those who seek the Kingdom of God are characterized by the opposites of the above list. They are unselfish, indifferent to wealth, simple of speech, humble. That describes my father. They do not discard what their parents taught them. They are grateful, reverent, men of normal human affections, self-controlled, lovers of God. Their life affirms their profession of faith. That sounds to me like Philip E. Howard, Jr. Dr. Frank Gaebelein, headmaster of Stony Brook School and later editor of *Christianity Today*, wrote in his introduction to my father's book *New Every Morning*,

> Philip Howard, who was my friend for many years, was an unusually disciplined Christian. Although in these essays, as in his other writings, he was careful to refer to himself only indirectly, there shines through their pages the transparent personality of a man of intellect and cultivation whose life was genuinely God-centered through Jesus Christ.

I have no recollection of any specific word my father spoke when I was very small, but I have a vivid sense of his comforting and sometimes awesome presence. Daddy was either at home or not at home, and the difference was very great. Sometimes I waited in the vestibule, peeping through the mail slot to see him come home from the office, up the porch steps, always dressed in a dark blue suit, white shirt, and conservative tie, always carrying a briefcase. When he opened the door I hugged his knees.

We know not a single word of anything Mary's husband Joseph ever said, but his silence was eloquent. As a faithful Jewish father he must have taught the Scriptures to the holy Child whom God had entrusted to him. In the temple in Jerusalem when Jesus was only twelve He gave remarkable evidence that He had learned His lessons thoroughly. We assume that Jesus learned also Joseph's trade of carpentry, and a skillful and conscientious carpenter He surely must have been. When He spoke of what He had seen the Father do, was He perhaps thinking not only of His Father God but also remembering his boyhood days of carefully watching Joseph, the one God had appointed to care for Him—watching him in his prayer life, his study of the Jewish Scriptures, his love for Mary his wife, his work with saw and adze and hammer?

My father's life as we witnessed it was more eloquent than anything he ever said. As an adult I have become aware of his simplicity, humility, and integrity, as well as of many other qualities of which a child would take no notice. We could not help noticing that he prayed, although we were not impressed, taking it for granted that that was what fathers did. He took as his pattern that of his Master, who prayed, "For *their sake* I consecrate myself, that they too may be consecrated by the truth" (John 17:19 NEB, italics mine). The responsibility of fatherhood was heavy upon him—how could he fulfill it unless he consecrated himself?—and it was too heavy to bear alone. "Take *my* yoke upon you and learn of me," said Jesus. My father tried to do just that. Like his Master he "rose a great while before day." He went downstairs in his robe (called a "wrapper" in those days) to kneel in prayer and study his Bible before breakfast. The difference it made to us to know that we had been thus prayed for every morning before we were awake was unperceived then, and only God can assess the long-term effects of those prayers throughout the rest of our lives.

"It was out of habitual rather than merely occasional early rising for prayer and Bible study," wrote Dr. Gaebelein,

> that Dr. Howard could write of an "early May morning . . . dark and still with an overcast sky and few stars," when the dawn "awoke that magnificent chorus of bird song . . . which seems like a paean of praise to the Creator . . . The symphony," he says, "was dominated by the sweet carols of the robins. As though at a signal from an unseen leader, in came the soft, low notes of the mourning dove, the intermittent

song of the red-eyed vireo, the bell-like tones of the wood thrush, the piccolo of the song sparrow, and even the raucous call of the crested flycatcher. Song seems the birds' first duty, even before feeding."

"One of the loveliest of natural phenomena is the morning star," wrote my father in the abovementioned book.

Often it has brought a sense of peace and renewed hope to the writer's heart as he has watched it just before dawn. Though he and all his associates work amidst the conglomerate din of street and factory all day long, yet, like many others, he has the blessing of a quiet, suburban home at night. And so there was one morning when, in the pre-dawn silence which is so conducive to meditation on the Word, he turned from the Word to the witness in the heavens and gazed in wonder at Venus, the morning star . . . untouched by earth's hurricanes, untroubled by its political turmoils, undisturbed by its international crises . . . It recalls Him who said, "I am . . . the bright and morning star . . . Surely I come quickly." (Revelation 22:16, 20).

"A Christian who is saturated with the Word," he said, "is likely to have a calm, wholesome outlook on life; to be kept steady in the path of God's will in either joy or sorrow, wealth or poverty; he is likely to be a pleasant companion, not voluble in aimless talk; and he will not be overly disturbed by world conditions."

When the youngest of us was a grown man he asked Dad for help in forming his own prayer list. He received this note:

1. Revise it occasionally.
2. Three columns:
   Organizations / People / Personal
3. A daily list, then another for each day, Monday, Tuesday, etc.
4. Any area of life where you find
   a. trouble
   b. mistakes
5. Don't limit prayer only to these things—pray for things you read about in the Bible.
6. Pray about the two most important decisions:

a. wife
   1) one who *wants* to go to the mission field, not just because you want to.
   2) pray *before* you become involved.
b. life work.

My father did not *push* us to prayer, he *led* us—first by that consistent example of being a pray-er himself, then by asking the blessing (a phrase he thought more accurate than "saying grace") at meals, and by gathering all of us together after breakfast for family prayers, as described in Mother's article. I do not say that we always followed willingly, or with anything like spiritual hunger or understanding, not until years later for most of us. But I do say that there was no hypocrisy on his part to pull the rug out from under what he tried to teach us. Children are keen as bloodhounds to sense that. He *believed* what he said. We could not have doubted that. And he lived by it.

It is significant to me that we never had anything that comes close to what nowadays would be termed *sharing* at family prayers. Nobody talked about how they felt about God. It was a brief and quite formal little meeting, always in the living room, away from the dishes and toast crumbs of the breakfast table. There was no variation in the order, no innovations, nothing "creative." A younger child passed out hymnbooks to all who could read. Everybody sang, the nonreaders memorizing hymns with astonishing speed. In addition to the great old hymns such as "O Worship the King," "Crown Him with Many Crowns," and "How Firm a Foundation," we loved gospel songs like "Jesus, Keep Me Near the Cross," "The Lily of the Valley," "It Is Well with My Soul," and, sung perhaps more than any other, "Trust and Obey," which might be called the practical as well as spiritual theme of our home.

❧ One day when Philip was in high school and had studied Latin, he was very eager to get on his bike and make contact with his friends, the fireman and engineer of the commuter train! When Dad asked what we should sing that morning Philip suggested NUNC DIMITTIS

(Lord, now lettest Thou Thy servant depart in peace)! ☙

Dave, at the age of three or four, stumped us all by requesting that we sing "the fuzzy hats." Finally someone remembered a hymnbook with pictures, one of them illustrating the Resurrection scene showing angels with haloes. So that was it —the "fuzzy hats"!

In times of deep distress I have been sustained by the words of hymns learned in family prayers. My friend Arlita Winston tells me her method for keeping depression and demons away: *sing hymns!* When three men were being taken out to be used as targets for bayonet practice in a Japanese prison camp, the men remaining sang "Abide with Me" to give the three courage to endure torture and death. Jesus sang a hymn with His disciples when He was on His way to Gethsemane. How thankful I have been in the dark hours that my parents saw to it that hymns became fixed in our minds and hearts, through what was to us at the time merely a family routine.

Bible reading followed the hymn singing. My father believed in reading *reverently* (we had to sit still—no fidgeting). He believed in reading *regularly* (twice a day aloud to us, at least once in private); he taught us to read it *all* (in private devotions he read the whole Bible more than forty times). He was strict, but he was also merciful to us, reading no more than a page or so a day from Hurlbut's *Story of the Bible,* an adequate spiritual dose for the youngest in the circle. Rarely did he expatiate on the short passage. He might occasionally put a question to a child to make sure we were paying attention, and if we were distracted or distracting others he stopped. Once he told Tommy that he must put down the pencil he was playing with. With his great dark-lashed blue eyes full of innocence Tommy ventured a timid defence: "But it *says* 'Jesus saves' on it!" It was a *Christian* pencil, wasn't it, surely permissible at prayers?

I tell this part of our story for the encouragement of fathers who do not find it easy to talk to anyone about spiritual things, let alone moderate a family discussion group. "I'm not really very spiritual," I have heard men say. "My wife's better at that." But a father is the priest in his home, held responsible by God for the spiritual training of his children. I am sure my father did not feel adequate in any sense of the word—far from it, in fact. He spoke of his own weaknesses with sorrow. But he knew his job. By God's grace he did it, without fuss or fanfare.

In Robert Burns's "Cotter's Saturday Night" we find a lovely picture of a worshipping family.

> The cheerfu' supper done, wi' serious face,
>   They round the ingle form a circle wide;
> The sire turns o'er w' patriarchal grace
>   The big *ha' Bible*, ance his father's pride . . .
> . . . .
> The priest-like father reads the sacred page,
> How Abram was the friend of God on high . . .
> . . . .
> Then kneeling down to heaven's eternal King,
>   The saint, the father, and the husband prays.

My father's prayers were notably simple. The blessing he asked at meals hardly ever varied: "Our Father, we thank Thee for this good food, and with this we ask Thy blessing, in the name of our Lord Jesus Christ. Amen." We children would smile at one another when Daddy began with "O God our Heavenly Father." We kept track of things, and noted that this opener was reserved (I feel sure he was unaware of this) for more serious occasions such as when we had company. His petitions at family prayers were things like, "Bless dear Mother, give her strength for her work today; bless Phil in his schoolwork, help Betty with hers—especially her arithmetic," etc., ending with, "In the name of our Lord Jesus Christ, who taught us to pray," whereupon we joined him in saying the Lord's Prayer.

After supper we were not excused from the table until our father had read a portion of Scripture—not Hurlbut's this time but *Daily Light*, that classic little collection of Bible readings for morning and evening. Prayer followed the reading. When it was time for bed either he or Mother would tuck the little ones in individually, singing a hymn and praying before kissing them goodnight. When Daddy came to tuck me in, he would sit on the bed, and I would often kneel, reaching up to put my hands on his knees. With his huge hands on mine he prayed for me. It is not hard for me, having had a father like that, to imagine what is meant by the prophecy of Isaiah concerning the Kingdom of Righteousness: "Each man will be like a shelter from the wind and a refuge from the storm, like streams of water in the desert and the shadow of a great rock in a thirsty land" (Isa. 32:2 NIV).

The biggest decisions of his life—his salvation, his marriage, his life's work—were made on the basis of eternal, not temporal value. When he accepted Uncle Charley's invitation to the S.S.T. he knew he would never come anywhere near being "comfortably off." What mattered infinitely more was being a faithful servant of God, and since his task as a father was a part of that service, he strove to set our hearts on the same transcendent goal. As he had covenanted with God to saturate himself in His Book, so he sought to teach us to love it. No one can make a child love anything, from spinach to sparrows to Scripture, but the parents' love for things exerts a powerful thrust in that direction (and I for one learned to love all of the above). It works both ways—a son whose father loves sports is likely to love sports; a son whose father hates work is likely to hate work. Because we heard the majestic cadences of the Authorized Version of the Bible read to us day after day, year in and year out, at home and in church and Sunday School and the Christian institutions we all attended, we learned, finally, to love the Bible, in spite of all the years when we shrugged and sighed and rolled our eyes and poked each other under the table and generally appeared to ignore what was supposed to be going on. Much more than we or our parents knew sank in by a sort of providential osmosis. Like other children, we learned radio commercials too ("Use Ajax, *bump-bum*, the foaming cleanser, *bump-bum*, floats the dirt, *bumpa-bum*, right down the drain, *bumpa-bumpa-bumpa-bum*," and "I'm Chiquita Banana and I—*come* to say—bananas have to ripen in a—*certain* way"), but Scripture occupies by far the larger share of the territory of our minds today.

Our parents gave each of us a nicely bound Bible of our own before we were ten years old, and encouraged us to read it for ourselves, underline, and make marginal notes. (On second thought, they probably said nothing at all about notes and underlining—we simply imitated what we saw.) We carried Bibles to Sunday School and church and looked up passages cited. We won the reference-finding competitions—Mrs. Stevens would belt out like a military officer, for example, "Romans 10:9!" and we would frantically whip through the pages and jerk triumphantly to our feet to read the verse aloud. As we reached the age where dinner table discussions became more lively and serious, we found that the Bible was always the reference point. Did God have anything to say about this matter? If so, let's find it, "for these commands are a lamp, this teaching is a light" (Prov. 6:23 NIV).

Paul the Apostle wrote,

> You are witnesses, as is God himself, that our life among you believers was devoted, straightforward and above criticism. You will remember how we dealt with each one of you personally, like a father with his own children, comforting and encouraging. We told you from our own experience how to live lives worthy of the God who is calling you to share the splendour of his own kingdom (1 Thess. 2:10–12 PHILLIPS).

That is how I see my father.

CHAPTER 12

FRUGALITY, HOSPITALITY, AND HEROES

By scrimping carefully the Howards had managed to put about two hundred dollars into a savings account. Then came the Great Depression. The bank closed, and the money was gone. Grandfather Gillingham came to the rescue and replaced what they had lost, but my father's salary, like almost everyone else's, was cut and it was even harder to balance the budget. Soup and macaroni-and-cheese were standard items on our menu. Steak was literally unheard of (I don't think I knew what it was till I was an adult), and ice cream and candy were major events in our childhood. We were aware of a very different standard when we went to Grandfather's house for Sunday dinners of roast beef and chocolate cake.

Mother's account goes on:

As the Bunkers used to sing, "Those were the days!" —of doing without. Without maids, without money, without new clothes, without a washer, drier, vacuum cleaner, radio, car—you name it, we didn't have it.

BUT we did have love in the family and we had three very dear children [Dave was born in 1928], and we always had enough to eat and enough hand-me-downs to keep us going.

"Mother!" moaned Bets one day, "You have on Aunt

Bertha's hat, Aunt Aline's dress, and Aunt Annie Keen's shoes!" I was dressed for some mildly festive occasion and had some idea I looked quite respectable!! I was a bit shaken in my idea!!

Washing blankets by hand in the big old soap-stone tubs in the chilly laundry and putting them through the hand-wringer was not easy, but when I compare my life at 103 with the life of Phil and Margaret at Nahanni [son and daughter-in-law in Northwest Territory, Canada, where they were missionaries to the Slave Indians] for so many years, my mouth is closed to complaints. ๛

When I was in the third grade, girls were required to take a sewing class. Our first assignment was to bring in a yard of gingham to make a bag to contain our work. I shook in my shoes at the thought of having to ask my parents for money— all of twenty cents—for the fabric. It simply did not occur to us to ask for money beyond our allowance, which was a nickel a week. We knew our parents "could not afford it," a phrase familiar to our ears then.

Yet we did not think we were poor, since there was always money to give away. Our parents were strict tithers, always setting aside for God at least a tenth of all that came in. That was not *their* money. It belonged to God. Some of the tithe was in a box in the drawer of the living room table—dimes which we were instructed to give to the poor unemployed who rang our doorbell almost daily, sometimes to sell pins and shoelaces, sometimes to ask for a dime or a sandwich. We understood that giving to them was giving to God, as was putting our pennies in the box in Sunday School.

My father's diary entry for August 10, 1939, gives a glimpse of a child's tithing:

> Ginny, five and a half, brought to breakfast her red barrel bank with pill box on top. She opened the pill box, took out a key, unlocked the bank, and gave me twenty-six pennies to take to Miss Stephen for the Belgian Gospel Mission. This amount was saved, K. told me, out of an allowance of six cents a week.

There was always money for God, money to buy books, enough to feed and clothe us—*very* modestly (I rarely had more than two pairs of shoes at a time—one for Sunday, one for school and play), and my clothes, as Mother said, had been worn by somebody else. Some were very beautiful and expensive, too nice for school, from a family we thought of as "rich."

We learned a strict frugality in the smallest things—turning off lights and water, being careful not to squeeze more toothpaste than we needed, saving the slivers of soap to be put into a small square wire basket on a handle. This was swished around in the hot water of the dishpan. If there were dishwashing products in those days we never heard of them. Plastics, of course, had not been invented, so we never *needed* a plastic bag. How much might be saved if a family today, anxious to save money and the environment, did not look on such things as necessities. We had waxed paper to wrap sandwiches in, but no paper towels, no foil, no Saran Wrap, no Baggies, no Ziplocs, no Tupperware, no Kleenex, and certainly no paper napkins (we had pure linen ones, handed down through generations). We never missed them! We managed, as most of the population of the world has always managed. Mother's rule was one her stepmother had taught her, and it is still the rule of my life: *wicked waste makes woeful want!*

There was always enough money for unpretentious hospitality. There is no mystery about this—God promises it. The Philippian Christians had been generous in their giving to the apostle Paul, and he likens their generosity to "a lovely fragrance, a sacrifice that pleases the very heart of God." So it always is, and always the promise is fulfilled, "My God will supply all that you need from his glorious resources in Christ Jesus" (Phil. 4:18–19 PHILLIPS).

My parents saw the entertaining of God's people as a great privilege and blessing to the family, so no matter what our economic condition, they contrived somehow to have a guest room set apart and always ready. The door to that room was kept closed when there were no guests, so it had its own special smell, a clean one of wallpaper paste, old wood, and furniture polish. There were a huge antique mahogany bed and a marble-topped bureau, a graceful oval table, and a big rocking chair. The menu for guests could not be much more than our usual family fare, but another place or two could always be set at the table.

When visiting speakers came to our church it was always assumed that the Howards would have them, and indeed the Howards were glad to, believing it to be clearly enjoined upon Christians to do so. "Give freely to fellow-Christians in want, never grudging a meal or a bed to those who need them," wrote Paul to the Romans (Rom. 12:13 PHILLIPS), and Peter's word was, "Be hospitable to each other without secretly wishing you hadn't got to be! Serve one another with the particular gifts God has given each of you, as faithful dispensers of the wonderfully varied grace of God" (1 Pet. 4:9–10 PHILLIPS). As I study the pictures of the houses my parents grew up in and compare them with the house we had, I know an occasional wistful thought must have crossed their minds, a flicker of a wish that they had a more commodious place for their guests, but such wishes never reached our ears.

My parents knew how important it was for us children to meet Christian men and women from all walks of life, to hear firsthand their stories of the faithfulness of God, and to enjoy the privilege of asking them questions. They did their best to persuade others in the church not to miss out on this blessing, but few understood what they were missing or saw it as a matter of obedience. Elders and bishops of the early Church had to be men of unimpeachable character, which meant, among other things, "*lovers* of hospitality."

Many people today consider it quite out of the question to invite guests often since it would require a major cleanup before they could be asked inside the door. Sometimes unexpected friends must be entertained on the porch because the living room isn't fit to be seen. The customary neatness of the house Mother kept eliminated, for the most part, this problem, but if things were not perfect she trusted friends to understand, without making a fuss for the sake of her pride.

"It is not a bad thing at all to have to tidy up the home for the coming of guests and to 'brief' the children ahead of time on the right behavior," wrote my father.

(Is there any home where none of this is ever necessary from one year's end to the other?) The presence of Christian friends or even strangers—unless they are very eccentric, self-centered, and thoughtless—should brighten the home and enlarge its outlook, as the guests tell of how the Lord has led them through the trials of life and of the work that they are doing for Him. It is a good thing for a family to be jolted out of its routine, and to look out beyond the four walls of its own home and the weekly routine of its own business, school, and church. If hospitality is withheld because "it is too much trouble" and costs too much, remember that we are commanded to show it, that it is to be given "without grudging," and that "there is that withholdeth more than is meet, but it tendeth to poverty" (Prov. 11:14). (*New Every Morning*, p. 95)

Mother wrote:

   When we were married one of the best presents we received was a guestbook. The first entry is the name of my dear "mother-in-love" and was in Brussels, dated August 30, 1922. The last name in the book is that of Eleanor Vandevort and the date is July 2, 1963, signed in Moorestown, New Jersey. Between those two dates are the names of people of twenty-four nationalities and people from forty-four countries. Among the friends who visited us while in Germantown I see the signatures of such people as Ernest Gordon, son of A. J. for whom Gordon College is named, I believe, George T. B. Davis of the Pocket Testament League, Wilbur Smith, Mrs. W. H. Griffith Thomas, Alice Gallaudet Trumbull Sparhawk, Betty Scott (later Stam, murdered in China by brigands), Charles Ernest Scott, her father, Allen MacRae of Faith Seminary, Ted Pudney of the Unevangelized Fields Mission, V. Atchinak of Beirut, William Pettingill, one of the editors of the Scofield Bible . . . and a host of others, some of whom I can't remember at all, but all of whom were a joy and delight to have in our home.

I remember Leland Wang of China whose motto was "No Bible, no breakfast." I was perhaps ten or twelve when he called me "the philosopher." Of course I did not forget that.

Then there was Mr. Vansteenberghe of the Belgian Gospel Mission, always exuberant and enthusiastic about everything in our home—my mother's cooking, our singing and piano playing, our schoolwork, my father's humor, Dave's haircut ("Oh brrruddah! How *chic*!"). Mr. Russell Abel of the South Pacific Mission told us of cannibalism and amused us by swinging us around in a chair. Mr. and Mrs. George Sutherland of the China Inland Mission taught us how to climb a mountain the way the Chinese coolies did, with a little bounce each time you put your foot down. Mr. L. L. Legters told us Indian stories from Mexico, and Miss Helen Yost told us Indian stories from Arizona. Ivan Bjornstadt of Norway electrified us with his booming baritone, and Arousiag Stepanian of Armenia sang in a high sweet soprano. She also told us her harrowing experience of the Turkish massacre when her relatives were all killed and she, a small child, was pulled from a ditch by Bedouins and taken to live in a tent in the desert. She still bore their tattooed mark.

Through these servants of God our imaginations were kindled, our ideals heightened. We had what every young person looks for—heroes, but of a sort too seldom found today, heroes well worth emulating. Their stories carried us far from our own small world, yet their values reinforced in vivid and dramatic ways exactly the values our father and mother were teaching us at home. At our own dinner table we saw and heard what it means to seek first the Kingdom of God, to give all to Jesus, to work for "gold, silver, and precious stones" rather than "wood, hay, and stubble."

CHAPTER 13

*T*HE
*L*ORD'S
*D*AY

We always went to Sunday School, and we always went to church. *Of course.* These are public means of grace, and there was never any discussion about our going, any more than about family prayers or any of the other regular habits our parents kept. Wherever the Lord's people were gathered together, there we were supposed to be. "The Church, its life, and the Holy Mysteries are like a tabernacle (tent) for the children, and they should be under it without leaving it. Examples indicate how saving and fruitful this is (such as the life of the Prophet Samuel)" (Theophan the Recluse, *Raising Them Right*, p. 30).

My father had been reared as a Presbyterian and my mother as an Episcopalian, but they chose for us, wherever we lived, the nearest church which they believed to be most faithful to the Bible. In that sense only—faithfulness to the Bible—could they be called narrow. My father's work in *The Sunday School Times* required a breadth of vision and understanding of many different denominations. My brother Phil recalls learning from our father an appreciation of the government of the Presbyterians, the reverence of the Episcopalians, the Bible knowledge of the Baptists, and the zeal of the Methodists. I remember my father's quoting,

For the love of God is broader
Than the measure of man's mind,
And the heart of the Eternal
Is most wonderfully kind.
—Frederick William Faber, 1862

The first Sunday School I remember was in a brand-new church building on Green Street. I was dressed in Sunday clothes, which meant a starched cotton dress, white cotton stockings, and "Mary Jane" shoes—black patent leather with a strap across the instep. I was thrilled to find not only small chairs, built exactly for us four- and five-year-olds, but even a low toilet in the bathroom. Daddy was always on the platform since he was the superintendent. We sat with our respective classes for the opening exercises and then went to classrooms where we were told Bible stories, given Sunday School papers with colored pictures, and taught a memory verse.

In church the whole family sat together in one pew. My father felt strongly about this. We were a family. We were meant to stand and sit and kneel before the Lord together, and, all objections notwithstanding (we raised many), I believe he was right. When Moses went before Pharaoh with God's message to let His people go so that they might serve the Lord their God, Pharaoh asked which ones would go. "We will go with our young and with our old, with our sons and with our daughters, with our flocks and with our herds will we go; for we must hold a feast unto the Lord" (Exod. 10:9 AV). Later, when Joshua read to the congregation what Moses had commanded, everybody was there, "the women, and the little ones, and the strangers that were conversant among them" (Josh. 8:35 AV). We read of Cornelius that he was "a devout man, and one that feared God *with all his house*" (Acts 10:2 AV, italics mine).

Sitting still was a point of doctrine. Judging by the ceaseless wriggling, twisting, getting up and down, and traipsing out to the restroom that one sees in churches today I gather that most parents assume it is impossible for little children to learn to sit still, even for an hour, and therefore cruel to expect it. To that I say *rubbish!* In the first place, I know it's possible—we learned it, and I know some children today who learn it. (Let no one suggest that the Howard children did it because they were phlegmatic types—every one of us has struggled to control our hereditary bundles of nerves!) In the second place, I believe it's wrong *not* to expect it, for in addition to being a fundamental lesson in a child's submission to the will of his parents, it is also the best place to begin to train mastery of the body. To control movement in obedience to parents enables a child to control movement later in obedience to his own will.

My father understood that he was in charge—head of the house, priest under God, charged with the solemn responsibility of his children's spiritual health for which he would one day have to answer. He could not force us to absorb the message, but he could put us in a position to hear it, never mind whether we understood it or not—how much did the disciples grasp of what their Lord taught? We would have liked to sit with friends, but it was wise that we were rarely allowed to do so, for we would have been even more irreverent and inattentive if not under our parents' eyes.

We who could read were expected to follow the service in the hymnbook, the prayer book (in the church where there was one), and the Bible, and there was plenty of sibling rivalry in finding the place. A certain amount of diversion for the youngest was permitted—he could sit on the kneeling bench and use the pew for a desk on which to draw pictures during the forty-minute sermons.

Sunday was a day set apart in other ways. When we did not go to the grandparents' we usually had guests. Mother cooked a real "Sunday Dinner," which, after the Depression, meant pot roast or chicken, gravy, potatoes, and a vegetable. We seldom had salad or rolls or extras of any kind, but there was dessert even if only canned fruit and store-bought cookies (Mother never was a baker). Occasionally we had the very special treat of a cake bought from the bread man who came every day with his horse and wagon and carried his basket to our door.

We did not change our clothes after church. This seems almost unbelievable today, especially in view of our relative poverty and the need to keep our one Sunday outfit respectable as long as possible. Our parents took the view that children behave according to the way they are dressed. They wanted us to think of Sunday as the Lord's Day, set apart in many ways as holy and separate from the other six days. We were limited to quiet activities—Bible games, books carefully chosen for Sunday reading, walks. If there was a young people's meeting at the church in the afternoon we went to that. Sometimes we went with Daddy to the evening service, although he did not insist on that since Mother stayed home with the baby. He went faithfully to Wednesday night prayer meeting, and as we grew older he would sometimes wistfully ask if anyone would like to go with him. To my regret now I think I went only a very few times. Prayer that costs us anything seems to be the last thing we learn.

A church as parochial organization is "a unity of place and not of likings, it brings people of different classes and psychology together" in the kind of unity the Lord desires.

My brother Tom, in his sketch of our father in the book *Heroes*, wrote,

He was very far from being at ease with the somewhat tatterdemalion set of sensibilities that eventually came to accompany Fundamentalist piety. Chattiness and rickety syntax in public prayers; pert or sentimental expressions of devotion in hymnody, or worse, rhapsodic protestations of self-consecration to God; flashy showmanship in evangelistic meetings; and the apparently *ad hoc* nature of a great deal of what went on in church services: these filled my father with anguished embarrassment.

It is hard to imagine a place less to my parents' tastes than the church we were attending when my father wrote a sketch (meant only for the family) of a certain Easter Sunday morning. If he knows now that I am putting it into print, I think he will not mind greatly, for it shows that the church was then, as it has always been, made up of nothing but *very* human beings, "beset by nature," to borrow the words of Evelyn Underhill, "and cherished by grace."

Mr. Conant in charge, a little late starting. Much ado about seating the regulars, the visitors, and the tots streaming up the stairs. Small, spring, straw hats blossom in the rows of seats, said hats being garnished with daisies, roses, asters, and even cherries (a little early, but never mind). A hymn is sung by all, with the time a little uncertain, as Jean is at the piano. Mr. C. announces a number by our "musical group," not a bad term, suggesting its loose arrangement, and aspirations if not brilliant successes. Silence, expectancy. Introductory flourishes on the piano. Silence. Now! Piano begins, followed by quavering moan from either saxophone or clarinet. (The group consisted of Janet, sax, Mr. McCoy, cornet, Jack and Ginny Norcross, clarinets, and Jean at the piano.) The wail joined and drowned by, successively, the cornet and the clarinets. Number proceeds, with the whole group sometimes in unison. Sundry sounds from babies at odd moments, dividing the attention, especially of the small fry, between the rear seats and the symphony up front. More singing, prayer, announcements. Then Mrs. Stevens' company. The customary pained and surprised expression on Mrs. S's face at the failure of certain rows, with snapping of fingers and nodding of head. Finally, on second song, a creditable performance. Now Mr. Conant, with chalk talk for kiddies, first; then a flannelgraph talk for the older scholars. Questions asked, some astounding answers from different quarters of audience, also some very good answers. Humorous side remarks from Mr. C. More grunts, squawks, halloos from babies in rear, and immediately a dozen pairs of small, bright, brown and blue eyes focused on the rear seats.

Well, it did go off well, and we had 212 present, which was fine! And the message of the resurrection and the Gospel were proclaimed once again, so we can be thankful. The humor is private, just for the family.

CHAPTER 14

A
HABIT
OF ORDER

*O*ur home was orderly. The grass was trimmed, the porch swept, wagons, bicycles, and sleds put away in the garage. Schoolbooks, shoes, papers, or toys did not adorn the front hall or the living room, towels were hung straight in the bathroom, the crisp linen doilies and dresser covers which my mother liked were always clean. A perfect home. Was it? Of course not. It could not have been impeccable at all times, but this is my impression and that of others who remember our home at all. As a child I took it for granted, but later when I came home from boarding school or college it hit me as soon as I entered the front hall—the freshness, the neatness, the sense of things being *placed*.

This was a visible sign of an invisible reality. Our parents believed in a God of order, Creator of a universe arranged in an orderly fashion, each thing in its appointed spot. When God gave instructions to Moses about the tabernacle He said, "Thou shalt bring in the table, and set in order the things that are to be set in order upon it; and thou shalt bring in the candlestick, and light the lamps thereof. And thou shalt set the altar of gold for the incense before the ark of the testimony," and so on, page after page, showing the Lord's love of order. Moses did just what he was told. "He put the table in the tent of the congregation . . . and he set the bread in order upon it before the LORD" (Exod. 40:4–5, 22–23 AV).

Men who qualified for leadership in New Testament churches (bishops, elders, and deacons) were those who managed their own households well and won obedience from their children. This gave them the right to speak openly on matters of the Christian faith (1 Tim. 3:4, 12; Titus 1:6). Women seeking authority in the church and home, and children showing no respect for parents, were signs of disorder.

Wherever they saw that God had given instructions my parents tried to follow them. I don't think nearly as much conscious effort had to be made then as seems to be needed now—conscious effort on my parents' part, I mean. The moral foundations on which their childhood homes were constructed had not been undermined as they have today. Certain prophecies from the book of Daniel seem appropriate for the time of this writing (and how often between Daniel's time and ours have they described the situation?)—a leader who will do what neither his fathers nor his fathers' fathers have done, devising plans against strongholds (the stronghold of the family, for example?), his heart set against the holy covenant so that he gives heed to those who forsake it. The temple profaned, the "abomination of desolation" set up in holy places, the people flattered when they violate the covenant, etc.

"But the people who know their God shall stand firm and take action. And those among the people who are wise shall make many understand, though they shall fall by sword and flame" (Dan. 11:32–33 RSV).

My father and mother took for granted the hierarchical order of the Christian home, a matter of far greater significance than where the schoolbooks and toys were kept. The husband was to be the head of the home, the wife in glad subjection to the office he was assigned. I doubt that this matter ever arose for discussion between them. It did not need to. They knew this was the way things were meant to be, the Scripture spelled it out clearly, and they accepted it without question. I have no doubt it was also exactly the way they wanted it to be.

Tom, in his book *Hallowed Be This House*, describes

the lovely rhythm of inequality as a mode of mutuality and joy. It is a state of affairs entirely repugnant to the imagination of hell, obsessed as that imagination is with questions of power, rights, and privilege. But questions of power, rights, and privilege have no meaning in this exchange here. The offering is real and free; the receiving is real and free.

When people decide to "wing it" and arrange things according to personal whim or comfort, they make a terrible mess, as Adam and Eve demonstrated when she took the initiative and Adam failed to protect her, as he was made to do, from that wrong choice. In recent years, with much discussion and protest about rights and equality, people have tried to rearrange just about everything, the word *traditional* has become a pejorative, and we have lost a great deal.

We were witnesses of the respect and love our parents had for each other. They were not overly demonstrative, but they called each other Dearie and we often saw them hug and kiss. When they went out my mother slipped her hand through my father's arm. We never once (I've checked with my brothers and sister about this) heard them raise their voices at each other or engage in a real argument. They presented a united front to their children, most particularly in matters of discipline (although I remember once being sent to bed without supper for some disobedience; Mother felt Daddy was too severe in this and brought me a bowl of porridge later). It was obvious to us that they liked and admired each other. Daddy often told Mother she was pretty and asked us if we didn't think so too. Well, now that he mentioned it, we did.

"Head of the house" did not mean that our father barked out orders, threw his weight around, and demanded submission from his wife. It simply meant that he was the one finally responsible. He took care of us. He was the provider and protector, making it possible for our mother to do her job full-time. She did the inside work, he did the outside, generally speaking. He also oiled hinges, changed washers, fixed things. Rarely did he dry dishes or bathe a child. He shut the windows and locked the doors and turned out the lights at night. He made us feel safe.

The smooth running of household wheels meant punctuality. My father had more clocks than a man needs. He wound them faithfully, balanced the mantel clock with bits of paper or cardboard under the corner, and synchronized them all with his thin gold Longines pocket watch which he checked weekly with the railroad clocks. If in a week's time he found it a few seconds slow or fast he adjusted it.

While some may regard strict punctuality as an amusing peculiarity or an irritating compulsion, it was a matter of Christian conscience to my father and hence to us. Lateness is stealing, he said. You are robbing others of their most irreplaceable commodity, time.

"A man's time can be given voluntarily, it can be bought, and it can be taken away from him against his will," he wrote in an editorial.

Some are habitually on time, others are habitually late; no one can be on time all the time, and no one needs to be always late. If five people have agreed to meet at a certain time and place, and one is fifteen minutes late, he has used up one hour in terms of man power, for he has taken away fifteen minutes from each of the others against their will. If they are wise, they will spend that time in reading or in some other useful way, but the latecomer ought not to presume on their good will if he can possibly help it. He might have the boldness to think—or to say—that they need to learn patience, that they are to be anxious in nothing—all of which is true, but he is not the man to tell them that. What he needs to remember, long before the appointment, is "rather, that no man put a stumblingblock or an occasion to fall in his brother's way" (Romans 14:13); that he has no right to waste others' time. Of course, no one can keep the phone or the doorbell from ringing just before he leaves home, nor can he prophesy what will happen on the way; but it is always a good rule to start just a little earlier than you think you need to . . .

Every Christian worker can discipline himself to be habitually on time, by careful management and foresight. It relieves other people of much anxiety, helps them not to waste time, and thus makes life easier for them. It is a matter of common honesty and Christian courtesy, and is in line with the injunction to "let all things be done decently and in order" (I Corinthians 14:40).

Being on time was also a practical necessity in our house, at least on weekdays, because my father took a commuter train into Philadelphia. This required an unvarying schedule for rising, eating breakfast, and having "Prayers." Both parents had to cooperate to make this work, and the habit was ingrained in all of us, though it was more painful for some than for others (Tom remembers being sent upstairs to hurry Jim, the youngest, and finding him seated in the middle of the floor "contemplating a shoe" or engaged in some equally fruitless endeavor).

Think of the alternatives. If everybody does that which is right in his own eyes there is no gathering together for a civilized breakfast, let alone for a quiet time in the living room afterwards. The frantic rush to find Father's briefcase, make school lunches, put on snowpants and galoshes (those dreadful things we wore with the metal clasps that were so hard for little hands to fasten), and get everybody out the door with the right lunch bags and schoolbooks, in time to be where they need to be, destroys peace for the rest of the day. We did our hustling first and had time to do the most important things "decently and in order."

The regularity of our schedule was one of the things we depended on, and though we did not know it at the time, it gave us a great security. Mother made it a rule to get meals on the table when we expected them to be there. Our little world could be counted on to stay the way it was, safe, "structured," and pretty much the same every day.

❧ Soon my little three-some were trekking nearly two miles up to Henry School. The long walk in all kinds of weather would be considered a very great hardship in these days of being taxied by long-suffering mothers, but it didn't seem to hurt my children. Besides we had no car then. Once in a while they had the thrill of being conveyed by Auntie Sue McCutcheon in their old Hupmobile. *❧*

As long as we lived in Philadelphia, we actually walked all the way home for lunch every day. We liked to. When we burst in the door there was Mother, and there was the hot soup. It was nice to smell the soup, and it was nice that Mother was always there for us. Always. When my father was asked to lead a tour group to Palestine for two whole months Mother would have loved to go along. She didn't. She stayed home with us. When he led another tour group to Alaska and when he traveled to Europe on business, Mother stayed home. It never occurred to us that it might be any other way. Today someone would be sure to point out that she "owed it to herself" to go on a cruise, or that she had "no life of her own." Nonsense, she would have replied—what do you call *this? This* is my life. Who'd ask for more? She never asked, and we were much the richer for it.

❦

An ordered home means not only an acceptance of God's arrangement of authority, and a conscientious regard for time, but also making sure that there is a place for everything. If there isn't, it probably means there are too many things. Some things must be got rid of. This requires regular inventory, sorting, and discarding or giving away. In our home there was a place for everything, and we understood that everything had to be put in its place. (For help in this, see Sandra Felton, *The Messies Manual*, Fleming H. Revell.) This takes endless repetition. There is no other way to train children.

It's much easier for the parents to pick things up themselves than to call the child, show him what he has left lying about, tell him where to put it, and see that he puts it there—and remind him the next time. "Much easier" only at the moment, I mean. "But I hate nagging!" we say, yet nagging is the lesser of two evils. It is a sort of "severe mercy," for the parents are sparing themselves endless pains when they take the trouble to teach, and, far more importantly, are sparing the children the frustration and confusion of disorder for the rest of their lives. The Scripture has a much gentler expression for that ugly word *nagging*—"precept upon precept, precept upon precept, line upon line, line upon line, here a little, there a little" (Isa. 28:10 RSV).

I use the word *nag* as it is commonly used today—repeating

what the child knows but has forgotten or has not heeded. I don't mean petty faultfinding or persistent scolding. The voice pitch and intonation make a great difference. A mother who uses a harsh tone is asking for argument and even defiance. She appears as the child's adversary rather than his helper. If she heard a tape recording of her customary tone in speaking to her children perhaps she would discover the main reason for their recalcitrance, or for the "breakdowns in communication."

When Mother was working in the kitchen she cleaned up as she went along. My father's desk was almost completely bare when he was not working at it. There were a blotter, a pencil tray (with all pencils sharpened and pointing in the same direction!), a few books neatly held by bookends, and perhaps a pad of paper, all placed parallel and squared with the corners of the desk. I used to leave things a little cockeyed after I had dusted, just for the amusement of seeing him straighten them, probably subconsciously, as soon as he came to the desk. Though we often teased him about this as we grew up, I am quite sure all six of us learned by his example, still follow it closely, and find our lives enormously simplified as a result. Was it primarily environment or was it heredity that most strongly influenced us in this regard? I'll leave that one to those better qualified than I to sort it out, but I was fascinated to discover an account of my father's meeting a man who had been office boy under both my great-grandfather and my great-uncle. The former had him dust all the books in the library every two or three months, at twenty-five cents an hour overtime. The latter had him buy a one-dollar Ingersoll watch and set it every morning at Bailey, Banks, and Biddle, Philadelphia's famous jewelers. Uncle Charley was determined to eliminate at least one excuse for the boy's coming in a minute or two late. He also had all the pencils sharpened every morning and *wiped off with a chamois* to remove the lead dust.

My father kept his tools on nails in the cellar or garage, each with a neat label over its proper place. Shoes, boots, galoshes, and rubbers were lined up in the bottoms of closets. Drawers were not meant to be a jammed jumble. We could *find* the can opener, the mending tape (Scotch tape had not been invented), the paper clips, the stamps or scissors because they were in the drawers where they belonged. If they weren't it was the fault of one of us, and we heard about it. It was a long, hard business learning to keep our own drawers as neat as theirs, but how thankful we are for the habit of uncluttered efficiency it established in all of us, I think, for life. Recently my oldest brother Phil visited us, and I watched him pack his small van for the long haul from Massachusetts to Alberta, Canada. He had built a nifty shelf inside the back door on which he placed suitcases, while small items he would need during the trip were stored underneath. On top of the van was a rack on which he arranged the cardboard boxes of family archives he was transporting for me to other family members en route, each box carefully wrapped in plastic and tightly taped. I teased him a bit about being the son of his father in the methodical way he went about the job, but of course to both of us there is an inevitability in it— wouldn't anybody do it this way? we ask, but a look at some of the crazily loaded vehicles one sees on the highways tells us they wouldn't.

CHAPTER 15

MORE BABIES

A block or so from our house was a sort of baby hospital, or perhaps a home for foundlings. I had been praying for a baby sister, and suggested to Mother that we might get one there. She explained that that was not the way she had gotten the rest of us. God could make babies grow inside of *her*. This sounded like a wonderful idea, and I did not worry about the details of the thing. I asked God please to grow me a sister.

In February of 1934, when Phil was ten, I seven, and Dave six, a manageably malleable clutch of chicks who were learning to do things our parents' way, our ordered life took a new turn. On one of the coldest days on record we woke to find Mother and Daddy gone, Aunt Alice fixing breakfast. A phone call later informed us of the birth of our baby sister, Virginia Anne, soon to be called Ginny. That was the day Dave chose to try to open a window that had been propped with a stick. Down came the sash with a crash, the glass shattered, the frigid winter wind blew in. We spent a very lonely, cold, and miserable day huddled under a rug beside the heating register in the downstairs hall, wishing that Mother would come home with the baby and that the man would come to fix the window.

෨   When I returned home I had some trouble with nursing and needed help. Bertha Kratz, a friend of a friend, came to help out. She was just out of the hospital herself and wanted a "light case." Ha! She had not been with us long when Dad got sick, Betty had tonsillitis, Phil had the measles, and poor Bertha was up and down those long flights of stairs a score of times a day. Later that year Phil, Bets and Dave all had mumps, stringing them out to the limit. In the end I got them too. Then came three tonsillectomies, the same three children. In those days we had to have quarantine signs on our front doors for any communicable diseases (this meant that only the breadwinner was allowed in and out). The yellow sign was on our door from April till August.

We got a breather for a couple of months and then Dave had to have a mastoid operation. Poor boy! He somehow got the idea that he was going to have his ear *cut off*! It wasn't till he was sitting up in bed while the doctor changed the dressings that he looked in the mirror and said, "Hey! I've still got my ear!" We have been eternally grateful to Mrs. Haines [mother of their old friend Meg] who came to our rescue at that time. She paid for Dave to have a nurse for a couple of nights and also helped with the expense of the hospital and the doctor. It has been exciting over the years to see how God met our needs in different ways. One day I was cleaning the guestroom and happened to open the Bible we kept on the table there. Out fell a fifty-dollar bill! To this day I have no idea where it came from.

July 22, 1935, was a scorching hot day but brought us much joy due to the safe arrival of a beautiful baby boy, Thomas Trumbull Howard. During his first year Dad was ordered by the doctor to work at the office only mornings and return home to bed to try to avoid possible tuberculosis. Little Tommy was his great delight at that time as I would bring him to sit on a sort of bedstand Dad had made to go across his legs so he could do his office work in bed. He was a very happy and smiling baby with great blue eyes, pink cheeks and dimples. He gave us both much to be thankful for! That same boy now looks so much like his Daddy that it is funny! And his gift of writing far exceeds any of his ancestors'!   ᎒

The following year marked two big changes. My parents bought their first car (I have always wondered what happened to that spiffy Buick Mother had had as a girl). It was a 1932 Plymouth, dark blue with yellow spoked wheels. I remember their sitting together at the library table in the living room, signing a paper, and then Mother, flourishing the pen, exulting, "The deed is *done!*" They found a garage nearby for rent at five dollars per month. It was a great luxury not to have to walk everywhere, or depend on Auntie Sue or Grandfather or the trolley cars for transportation.

The other change was a move.

᎒ For several years we had been praying to be able to sell our house. The neighborhood was getting more and more run down and the family was increasing. The pocket-handkerchief-size back yard of 103 W. Washington Lane was not much of a place to play. The boys had sled wagons and scooted up and down the street and sometimes coasted down the hilly part of McCallum Street, endangering not only their own lives but that of innocent old ladies and small tots, so it was a wonderful relief to move to 29 East Oak Avenue, Moorestown, New Jersey in 1936.

Dad had mentioned to Mr. Bill Richie of the Scripture Gift Mission, with offices on the same floor with the Sunday School Times, that we were very anxious to get away from Germantown and into a more quiet neighborhood. It turned out that the house next door to the Richies was for rent.

This big old house was a real joy. It was very spacious —seventeen rooms altogether! And a big yard with two garages (the assorted bikes, express wagons, sled wagons, tricycles, sleds, etc. took up one of these). Soon there was a nice sand box in the back yard. There were lovely trees—dogwood and tulip poplar and a big copper beech in the front yard, a marvelous place for playing with toy cars, making roads and farms, bridges and houses. Wonderful hours were spent in its beautiful shade and imaginations became more fertile as the years went by. It seems to me most children today don't know how to really PLAY, but ours had this opportunity and made the most of it.

The one drawback to this house was that there was only one bathroom, but we managed well and it was nice to have plenty of bedrooms. A tiny room in the front held the baby's crib and not much else. Next to it was a big room just right for the two girls of the family. Our room was back of that. A nice guestroom was across the hall. This served for a hospital room when anyone was sick. Back of that was a smaller room which was first Davy's and then Tommy's. A big enclosed upstairs porch was young Phil's choice. He was the outdoorsman! I have gone into his room in the winter and there he was, all the windows open wide and his bed pulled right under one of them and snow pouring in onto the bed. I would demur, only to be told that he was acclimatising himself to the cold because he planned to go to the Arctic when he was a man!!!! He read everything he could get his hands on about the north—all of James Oliver Curwood's books, for instance. Well, it all paid off, didn't it?

There were four huge bleak rooms on the third floor which were used mostly for storerooms till we had another addition to the family a few years later.

Downstairs were a living room, study, dining room, kitchen, and laundry. Back of the study was a glass-enclosed room underneath Phil's glass-enclosed bedroom. This was a sort of catchall and playroom. Tuck, our well-behaved little fox terrier, slept there.

There was a big front porch which also came along the side of the house, too, a perfect place for our babies to play and sit in their "rocking duck" in the sun! When small Jim was old enough for that I would put him out there, bundled up in a woolly snowsuit. I'd hear the duck rocking furiously for a long time. Then it would stop suddenly, then off again full speed, then slower and slower, another spurt of speed, another slowing down and finally silence! He was asleep. This was a regular routine each day. But I haven't even got him born yet! I am ahead of my story. ❧

CHAPTER 16

A
FATHER'S
TENDERNESS

The prophet Hosea gives a beautiful description of the fatherly care of the Lord:

> I myself taught Ephraim to walk, I took them in my arms; yet they have not understood that I was the one looking after them. I led them with reins of kindness, with leading strings of love. I was like someone who lifts an infant close against his cheek; stooping down to him I gave him his food (Hos. 11:3–4 JB).

Love, protection, patience, kindness, tenderness, provision —it is not hard to put my father into that picture. His babies fit quite neatly into his big hands as he lifted them close against his cheek. Even the "reins of kindness" and the "leading strings" call up a memory. Mother had had a little leather harness made for Phil in Belgium—"reins of kindness" to keep him from falling overboard on the voyage home.

I love this stanza from Henry F. Lyte's hymn, "Praise, My Soul, the King of Heaven,"

> Fatherlike, He tends and spares us,
> Well our feeble frame He knows;
> In His hands He gently bears us,
> Rescues us from all our foes.

As Christ's submission to His Father meant also His submission to the needs of His disciples, so a father's submission to a Heavenly Father means submission to the needs of his children, in other words, sacrifice and humble service, always the conditions of Godlike authority. "I am among you as one who serves," Jesus said (Luke 22:27 rsv).

Martin Luther wrote,

> Our natural reason looks at marriage and turns up its nose and says, "Alas! Must I rock the baby? wash its diapers? make its bed? smell its stench? stay at nights with it? take care of it when it cries? heal its rashes and sores? and on top of that care for my spouse, provide labor at my trade, take care of this and take care of that? do this and do that? and endure this and endure that? Why should I make such a prisoner of myself?"
>
> What then does Christian faith say to this? It opens its eyes, looks upon all these insignificant, distasteful and despised duties in the spirit, and is aware that they are all adorned with divine approval as with the costliest gold and jewels. It says, "O God, I confess I am not worthy to rock that little babe or wash its diapers, or to be entrusted with the care of a child and its mother. How is it that I without any merit have come to this distinction of being certain that I am serving thy creature and thy most precious will? Oh, how gladly will I do so. Though the duty should be even more insignificant and despised, neither frost nor heat, neither drudgery nor labor will distress me for I am certain that it is thus pleasing in thy sight."

Insignificant, distasteful, despised duties—all adorned with divine approval, as with the costliest gold and jewels. I think my father and mother saw *through* the duties to the jewels, saw their work as the priceless privilege of cooperation with God and their children as *His*, lent to them for a time (such a *short* time), and their home as a small cosmos representing the City of God, instead of seeing the whole scene as a cartoon in a Christian magazine recently depicted it—the mother disheveled and harried, the children wildly out of control, the cat and dog tearing each other's ears off, the father a helpless spectator.

In stark contrast to this cartoon is the pattern my father set, very like that of Paul's instructions to Titus:

Teach the older men to be temperate, worthy of respect, self-controlled, and sound in faith, in love, and in endurance . . . Similarly, encourage the young men to be self-controlled. In everything set them an example by doing what is good. In your teaching show integrity, seriousness, and soundness of speech that cannot be condemned, so that those who oppose you may be ashamed because they have nothing bad to say about us (Titus 2:2, 6–8 NIV).

Christian men who earnestly want to be faithful fathers will perhaps find the cartoon in the magazine dismayingly like some of the scenes in their own homes, and be aware that they fall far short of the high standard described in the letter to Titus. But God never issued instructions which He is not prepared to enable us to follow. The contrast between the actual and the ideal, between the reality and the holy standard, is bridged by the grace of God, and by our prayers for the application of that grace. He is our Savior and our Helper. As Father of fathers, He longs to show us His way, to lift us when we fall, to forgive us when we sin, to give us the supernatural power to do that which we cannot do naturally.

It is sad to read that the average father nowadays spends three minutes per week with each child. Home, frankly, is just "not his scene." He'd rather be elsewhere. What does he do with the rest of his time? Is it a relentless frantic scramble to earn money five or six days a week, with a frantic scramble on weekends to "relax" and enjoy *himself*, often in expensive and sometimes dangerous ways? Can this really be what God wants for Christian families? If there were the willingness to be content with less money, fewer activities which eat into the budget and take the family away from home, fewer possessions; if there were the willingness to "be content with such things as you have," would we not sooner find the truth of God's Word, "A man's real life in no way depends upon the number of his possessions" (Luke 12:15 PHILLIPS)? The willingness to be and to have just what God wants us to be and to have, nothing more, nothing less, and nothing else, would set our hearts at rest, and we would discover that the simpler the life the greater the peace.

In Thomas Merton's autobiography, *The Seven Storey Moun-*

tain, he describes as among the most remarkable people he ever knew a French peasant family with whom he and his father boarded for a time. M. Privat was a short man, broad, of great strength. He wore a black broad-brimmed hat which "gave his face an added solemnity when his sober and judicious eyes looked out at you peacefully . . . His little wife was more like a bird, thin, serious, earnest, quick, but also full of that peacefulness and impassiveness which, as I now know, came from living close to God." Merton was only a boy, and forgot most of the details about this couple, but remembered

> their kindness and goodness to me, and their peacefulness and their utter simplicity . . . They were saints in that most effective and telling way: sanctified by leading ordinary lives in a completely supernatural manner, sanctified by obscurity, by usual skills, by common tasks, by routine, but skills, tasks, routine which received a supernatural form from grace within, and from the habitual union of their souls with God in deep faith and charity.
>
> Their farm, their family, and their Church were all that occupied these good souls; and their lives were full.

My father once spoke in chapel at the Stony Brook School on Paul's word, "Make it your ambition to lead a quiet life, to mind your own business and to work with your hands" (1 Thess. 4:11 NIV). Imagine choosing that piece of advice for a bunch of schoolboys! But it was the rule he lived by and had found it the secret of peace. He wanted the boys to have it.

A quiet life meant that Daddy was at home more evenings than he was out. He went to Sunday evening service and Wednesday evening prayer meeting at church. He had a few speaking engagements and board meetings and an occasional social evening (these were very rare), but most evenings he was at home, sitting in his armchair in the corner of the living room, ankles resting on a footstool, manuscript or book in hand, and once in a while a little child on his lap.

The diary he kept for the brief period of August 1939 to February 1940 is, by usual standards, quite unremarkable:

Friday, Sept. 29. Office all day. Went out to the barber's at noon. Home for supper. Had happy time with K. and the children. We got ice cream about nine o'clock. We sat in the living room reading different books and magazines.

Sunday, Oct. 1. We all went to Sunday School and church this morning. At the men's class I told them I must give up teaching for the time, according to Dr. Erdman's orders. Many expressed regret. John McNiney could hardly speak, and said he didn't know what to say. We had communion service in church. After dinner we all sat in the living room, reading and singing, while K. played the piano.

Unremarkable to most. Quite remarkable to me as I read it fifty years later, discovering in its neatly penciled pages what seems a rarity in America today, the portrait of a quiet, honest, ordered life, and the combination of godliness and contentment which the Bible calls "great gain."

Vignettes from the diary show his tender delight in his children. After weeks without the family (because of the polio epidemic we had stayed at our summer home in New Hampshire while he had to go back to work): "Had a fine family reunion at supper time. K. met me at station with Tommy and Ginny [who were then four and five]. Ginny ran to train to hug me; K. says Tommy danced up and down in the car saying, 'My dear daddy, my dear daddy!' "

On a Sunday in October the diary mentions the sermon in church, then "a happy time at dinner," a visit to a sick lady, a walk with oldest son Phil and Phil's friend Albert, searching for a pond where there were said to be ducks.

Found no pond and consequently no ducks. Saw a marsh hawk, doves, crows, juncos, heard myrtle warblers and white-throated sparrows and pheasants . . . Went upstairs after supper and came upon one of those lovely family pictures that delight my heart. Tommy sat in the rocker in Betty's room, wearing Ginny's new little round red hat, and looking up at Betty as she combed her hair. They were singing together, "The Old Rugged Cross."

My father's recreation nearly always included his children. We could count on his doing something with us on Saturday afternoons—walks to the Walnut Lane Bridge or to Thomas's Place in Fairmount Park where he would miraculously "find" Saltines in the hollow of a tree. A Saltine was a treat for us in those days, and very exciting when extracted from a tree or perhaps from an unsuspecting boy's pocket. Daddy took us to the zoo, the Planetarium, the Franklin Institute, long rides to the New Jersey Pines or the shore where he taught us to love silence and the smell of pine woods and salt marshes.

Wherever we went he watched for birds. He wanted so badly to give to each of us the love he had had for these beautiful creatures ever since his teen years. I lost a great deal by responding only halfheartedly to his offers of prizes for the numbers of species identified—a Peterson guide book, a pair of field glasses. I was rather like a friend who said he could identify forty birds, but thirty-nine of them were robins. My brothers did much better, earning the prizes and several learning to imitate birdcalls quite well, but none with the perfection of our father. He gave to each of us a special bird-call which he used instead of our name if we were at a slight distance away, in another room, across the street, or in the back yard. Mother's was the chickadee, mine was the wood pee-wee. As I write, it is springtime on the coast of Massachusetts, and the wood pee wee has come back for the summer. From time to time the tiny three-note call rings pure and clear from the oak wood next to our house, and I want to run and say, "Yes, Daddy?"

We learned to walk quietly in the woods, stand with hands behind our backs so as not to frighten the birds with sudden movements. We learned to recognize the nests and flight patterns of at least a few birds, and to hear their calls and songs (people do have to be *taught* to hear things—I learned this again when I lived in the Amazon rain forest and would have missed many jungle sounds if my Indian friends had not called them to my attention).

Birds often figured in my father's editorials

Feathered pilgrims of the sky cover thousands of miles over land and water each spring and fall without compass, map, or radar, yet they fly unerringly to and from their winter quarters and their nesting grounds. The ornithologists have sought diligently for the reasons for the mass flights and for the principles that guide the birds, and have advanced a few explanations which are not entirely convincing. The simplest solution of the problem is that the birds travel by God-given instincts and powers of observation far surpassing man's.

The essay goes on to describe a flight of geese he saw flying toward the South Jersey shore one morning in March, honking and yapping like dogs.

> Flying at an altitude of perhaps four hundred feet, they were visible for a short space through the flying snowflakes, and it was thrilling to see them steadily beating their way through the storm . . . The observer wondered whether their strange gabbling meant something, whether some were complaining about the hardness of the way, whether others were saying they must keep on to that marshy bay or thoroughfare just sixty miles further. (They could easily cover the distance in an hour and a half.) The watcher was made mindful again, as often before, of God's marvelous care of the birds and of His skill in guiding them through the pathless sky.
>
> Every child of God is of more value than a flock of twittering, quarrelsome English sparrows or a flight of geese moving on mighty wings. He can expect his Heavenly Father to feed, clothe, and guide him as surely as He does the birds. And many lessons can be learned from the birds' obedience— whether conscious or unconscious—to God's laws.
>
> Bird-watching is a pleasant and inexpensive hobby, which may be enjoyed any time, anywhere; but it is more than that, for the birds are used in Scripture to illustrate spiritual truth. The Lord Jesus said, "Take a good look at the wild birds, for they do not sow or reap, or store up food in barns, and yet your heavenly Father keeps on feeding them. Are you not worth more than they?" (Matthew 6:26, Williams). (*New Every Morning*, pp. 24–26)

One day he took us to the U.S. Naval hangar in Lakehurst, New Jersey, to see the dirigible *Los Angeles*, and we were allowed to go into the cabin. I remember the wide seats of red plush, a luxury far surpassing the green plush train seats so familiar to us (not to mention the narrow, cramped plane seats of today).

He knew how to play with small children. He would let two of us ride on his size twelve feet, hugging his calves, or get down on all fours and ride us around the dining room table. He wrote "The Burlington County March," a catchy little tune that toddlers loved to march to as he played the piano. He did sleight of-hand magic (swallowing a penknife, finding pennies in our ears) and handkerchief tricks. He could produce a snappy rhythm with the fingers of one hand on the knuckles of the other. Lorraine Winston, missionary in France, wrote to Mother after my father died:

> The children speak often of Uncle Phil. Johnny, who was just about four when he saw him last, still talks about his magic tricks, and said to me one day that he didn't think he would mind dying and going to be with Jesus, "cause Uncle Phil is there already." It seems to have made heaven a really home-like place to him. Of all the people who come and go through this house, Uncle Phil has left the happiest memories in the children's hearts, and that speaks volumes. It was that sort of attraction that children felt for the Lord, I'm sure, and Uncle Phil had that aspect of the Lord's loveliness in a very great measure.

CHAPTER 17

A MOTHER IS A CHALICE

*B*efore my much-prayed-for sister was born Mother sat down in the rocker in the bay window of the front bedroom and began to knit. The needles were very small, and the wool was very fine. I had often seen her knit, but not with needles and wool such as these. I asked what she was making. It was tiny little shoes—not "booties," but in the style of "Mary Jane" shoes. She made a little strap across the instep, secured with a small pearl button. For whom? I wanted to know, and listened with wonder as she explained that someday soon I would have a new brother or sister who was right now growing inside of her. The shoes were for the baby.

During the next weeks I learned of the mysteries of caring for a new baby. Daddy set up the crib which Davy had outgrown, and came home with a "bathinette," a folding table with a drop-top for changing the baby's diapers, underneath which was a rubber pouch with a drainage tube—the baby's bathtub. There were pockets attached to a sort of dashboard which Mother began to fill with cotton swabs, baby oil and powder, safety pins, a special baby washcloth, and soap. I was enthralled. Then one day she called me to help her tear up old pajamas into eight-inch squares. These, too, were for the baby—disposable liners to put inside the Birdseye diapers for the times when Mother expected a bowel movement. What happiness I felt in being allowed to help with such exciting things!

Scripture teaches that older women have the responsibility of teaching younger ones to love their children. Love certainly involves attention to basic bodily needs, and in allowing me to share in her preparations Mother was teaching me things I would remember perfectly when my own child came. She being the youngest in her family had not participated in the care of a baby, and her own mother was of course long dead by the time her children were born. Children don't come with a set of instructions, so mothers need help. It is sad that so few older women think of offering it to bewildered young mothers who hardly know where to begin. It's sad, too, that the young ones seldom think of asking.

I did not know the things Mother kept in her heart and pondered—things of far greater consequence than the physical care of the coming child. The fear of God was in her heart, the deep awe of receiving a gift, the sense of her own inadequacy to be to this child all that she ought to be.

The Hebrew midwives also feared God, and when the king of Egypt ordered them to kill all newborn Hebrew boys they disobeyed. They let the boys live. In preparing for the coming of a strong deliverer for His enslaved people, God began with these devout women. He rewarded their obedience by giving them families of their own. Pharaoh's next order was that the Hebrew boys must be thrown into the Nile. God chose a Levite woman with the courage to defy the king's edict and hide her son for as long as possible—three months. Then, entrusting him utterly to God, she (in a manner of speaking) "threw" him into the Nile, but in a nice basket which she had made and waterproofed.

An anonymous writer declared,

> There is no nobler career than that of motherhood at its best. There are no possibilities greater, and in no other sphere does failure bring more serious penalties. With what diligence then should she prepare herself for such a task. If the mechanic who is to work with "things" must study at technical school, if the doctor into whose skilled hands will be entrusted human lives,

must go through medical school . . . how much more should the mother who is fashioning the souls of the men and women of tomorrow, learn at the highest of all schools and from the Master-Sculptor Himself, God. To attempt this task, unprepared and untrained is tragic, and its results affect generations to come. On the other hand there is no higher height to which humanity can attain than that occupied by a converted, heaven-inspired, praying mother.

One day when I was thirteen I came home from school as usual, put down my books, and went to find Mother. She was in the kitchen making something for supper. I stood by the corner of the table watching her. She was unusually quiet. Finally she looked up and smiled.

"Which would you like to have—another brother or another sister?"

Something inside me seemed to plummet. I had "helped to raise" Tommy and Ginny, and they were now four and five. Five children were enough. Mother would be forty-one when the next was born. I did not know what to say. I suppose I said I'd rather have a sister, to make an equal number of girls and boys.

At thirteen I could not have imagined the hard struggles Mother must have had with the Lord during those next months. There was no such thing as amniocentesis in those days, and abortion was a thing not named among Christians. Of course she would not have entertained for one moment the thought of either. Her doctor did not ask the question that is now routine in prenatal examinations: Do you wish to continue this pregnancy? It was all very simple. She was pregnant. She was going to have a baby. Nothing was negotiable. But simple doesn't always mean easy.

Children, the Bible says, are a gift, a blessing, a heritage from the Lord, "the fruit of the womb a reward. Like arrows in the hand of a warrior are the sons of one's youth. Happy is the man who has his quiver full of them!" (Ps. 127:3–5 RSV). Mother and Daddy believed that and believed He would give them just what He wanted them to have, which is always the best. While Jim was not, I believe, their only "unplanned" baby, Mother told me in later years that it was indeed a shock to find herself pregnant with Number Six.

Mother's story takes up the thread again.

ᴄᴅ It was a sultry, thunderstormy night, that July twentieth of 1940. Dad and I were sitting out in the back yard of Oak Avenue, to get a breath of cool air, when I began to realize that our sixth child was soon to make his appearance. Nineteen long laborious hours later, with our dear friend Bertha Kratz hovering over me, wee Jim entered this "scene." The ten days that followed must have been among the hottest in history. Thunderstorms raged every day. Bertha arrived at the hospital one day when I had the baby with me (she was trying to keep her hand on things at home where another helper, Beatrice, was doing her best). He had a burning fever and, blessings on her, I believe she really saved his life as she pumped fluids into him, saying he was completely dehydrated. The nursery nurse had assured me there was nothing the matter with him when I had spoken to her of how burning hot he was. How thankful I am for Bertha's presence! ᴄᴡ

I walked down Oak Avenue and up Mill Street to the bus stop every day and rode to Mt. Holly, then walked some more in the hot sun to the hospital to visit Mother. She was always pleased to see me, pleased to show me the baby, but I remember how she suffered with the heat, lying there on the white sheets, sucking crushed ice, and fanning herself with a Chinese paper fan.

ᴄᴅ In those days mothers stayed in the hospital at least ten days and when they returned home they were pampered for another week or so, which I always enjoyed. They were not allowed to climb stairs for a time. When I came home from the hospital my oldest son, Phil, then seventeen, was standing by and carried his mother upstairs! ᴄᴡ

A mother is a chalice, the vessel without which no human being has ever been born. She is created to be a life-bearer, cooperating with her husband and with God in the making of a child. What a solemn responsibility. What an unspeakable privilege—a vessel divinely prepared for the Master's use.

Sigrid Undset, in her great Norwegian novel *Kristin Lavransdatter*, describes a mother, seated at sunset on a hill overlooking her manor house, reflecting on her responsibilities as wife and mother:

> She had worked and striven—never till tonight had she known herself how she had striven to set this manor on its feet and keep it safe—nor all she had found strength to do and how much she had compassed.
>
> She had taken it as her lot, to be borne patiently and unflinchingly, that all this rested on her shoulders. Even so had she striven to be patient and to hold her head high under the burden her life laid on her, each time she knew she had again a child to bear under her heart—again and again. With each son added to the flock, she had felt more strongly the duty of upholding the welfare and safety of the house—she saw tonight, too, that her power to overlook the whole, her watchfulness, had grown with each new child she had to watch and strive for. Never had she seen so clearly as this evening what fate had craved of her and what it had granted her, in giving her these seven sons. Over again and over again had joy in them quickened the beating of her heart, fear for them pierced it—they were her children, these great lads with their lean angular boys' bodies, as they had been when they were so small and plump they could scarce hurt themselves when they tumbled in their journeys between the bench and her knee. They were hers, even as they had been when, as she would lift one of them from the cradle up to her breast for milk, she had to hold up its head, because it nodded on the slender neck as a bluebell nods on its stalk. Where they might wander out in the world, whithersoever they might fare, forgetful of their mother, she felt as though for her their life must still be an action of her life, they must still be as one with herself as they had been when she alone in all the world knew of the new life which lay hidden within and drank of her blood and made her cheeks pale. Over again and over again had she proved the sickening sweating terror when she felt: now her time was

come again, now again was she to be dragged under in the breakers of travail—till she was borne up again with a new child in her arms; how much richer and stronger and braver with each child, never till tonight had she understood.

When parents receive a child from the hand of God they receive a life to be shaped and moulded—most of that shaping and moulding taking place, psychologists say, during the first seven years (and some say by far the most impressionable years are the first three). Their job, in the words of Janet Erskine Stuart, is "to give a saint to God." Who is sufficient for these things? This small package of living flesh, with their blood coursing through its tiny veins, their features alarmingly recognizable on the wizened face; real, workable fingers, ten of them, capable of a damp, hot, strong grip on one of theirs; lungs which can produce the most heartbreakingly soft coos and unbearably harsh cries; skin so smooth, so silky, so tender you want to weep when you touch it. And they are responsible for this? Solely responsible—to give a *saint* back to God!

There has been no preparation which seems nearly adequate for this cataclysmic upheaval of their lives. A boy and a girl became a husband and a wife, and suddenly they are a father and a mother, overnight as it were, without anything to ready them for the awesome task of fashioning the destiny of a soul. The awareness of inadequacy frightens the life out of many. One man told a TV audience he panicked. He wanted to run. " 'Well, yeah,' I said. 'He's cute, but if you want me I'll be down at the bar.' " Down on his knees would be a better place to go. The One who fashioned the child and gave him to these two people is ready to give the wisdom they know they lack, if only they ask.

The process of shaping the child, as Kristin saw, shapes also the mother herself. Reverence for her sacred burden calls her to all that is pure and good, that she may teach primarily by her own humble, daily example.

I wonder whether Mother still had diapers and baby bottles that the rest of us had used, or whether she had to buy new ones for the latest little surprise. I don't remember. But once again there were formulas to prepare (Mother had tried hard to breastfeed her babies, without success). Once again there were the sterilizing pot and the array of shining bottles, the funnel and the cans of evaporated milk spread out on the white enamel kitchen table. Once again we washed Birdseye diapers in the old machine and put them through the wringer by hand and pinned them to the clothesline outdoors and brought them in and folded and folded and folded them. So, like Mary the mother of Jesus and Kristin Lavransdatter and all the mothers of the world, my mother was again (or rather still) a "quiet servant of necessity," doing the work no one would notice or thank her for—no one, that is, except Him to whom it could be offered as a daily sacrifice of love.

The apostle Paul used a curious expression in his first letter to Timothy. A woman is "saved through motherhood"—if she continues in faith, love, and holiness, with a sober mind. There are many interpretations of these words. I believe it means at least this much: that she will be kept in the path of safety, not by taking the offices of men, but by performing the functions assigned by the Lord, provided she continues in faith, love, holiness, with a sober mind (is there anything which can sober a woman's mind more effectively than motherhood?). Some are never granted the gift of motherhood. Some refuse it. To those to whom it is granted, humble obedience to its demands is their very "salvation," the way to joy and peace. A mother cannot "save" herself. Like Jesus who refused to come down from the cross, she cannot save herself because she is "saving" others, giving her lifeblood for them. Like Him, she can save herself only by losing herself. "Whoever loses his life for My sake will find his true self." Those to whom the privilege of childbearing is not given are "saved" by accepting the will of God in this as in all else, and by carrying out the work He does assign.

A talented woman was asked by a friend, "Why have you never written a book?"

"I am writing two" was the quiet reply. "I have been engaged on one for ten years, the other five."

"You surprise me!" the friend said. "What profound works they must be!"

"It doth not yet appear what they shall be," said the

woman, "but when He makes up His jewels, my great ambition is to find them there."

"Your children?"

"Yes, my two children. They are my life's work."

And so for Mother, we six were her life's work. She asked for no other.

CHAPTER 18

SACRIFICIAL AUTHORITY

"I fall on my knees before the Father (from whom all fatherhood, earthly or heavenly, derives its name)" (Eph. 3:14–15 PHILLIPS).

It is the apostle Paul speaking. Given the tremendous burden of the care of all the churches, he, a true father in the deepest sense, falls on his knees before Him for whom all fatherhood is named, to intercede for his spiritual children. My father, often wrapped in a steamer rug (a wool blanket which the deck stewards of the old ocean liners used to tuck up around passengers basking on deck chairs) against the predawn cold, fell on his knees daily beside a threadbare old armchair in his little study to pray for his children. This was his primary duty, his priestly duty, and he gave it first place in his day.

When we give the first part of the day to Bible reading and prayer, we get our own hearts into tune with God and we can then work more smoothly and efficiently. It is like the tuning of an instrument before the symphony that there may be no discord. As we wait before God, He may point out to us sins that need to be confessed and forgiven, weaknesses that need to be overcome, failures that need to be corrected, and when these are made right we are ready for His use. As we consciously cast our cares upon Him, our minds are relieved of the burden of our own troubles and set free for dealing with the problems of our own work or those of others who may come to us for help. (*New Every Morning*, p. 127)

Authority is for many people an "off-putting" word, and no wonder, for in its crude and unregenerate state it is often coercive and domineering. I don't think any of us felt that our father's authority was of that kind. He was meek, in that he understood his place in God's economy. He submitted to God first—in fact, his acceptance of his fatherly responsibilities was evidence of that submission. He understood the Christian principle of human relationships, radically different from the world's, the principle of the crucified Christ, "my life for yours." Misunderstanding and misuse of the God-given authority of husbands and fathers have led to all sorts of chaos and suffering, not the least of which is the rebellion of women against men and, consequently, against their own created nature of femininity. (For further discussion of this, see my *Let Me Be A Woman* and *The Mark of a Man*.)

The responsibility of men to care for and protect women is an ancient and deep-seated understanding, beautifully illustrated in a story William Oddie tells in his *What Will Happen to God?* (on feminism and the reconstruction of Christian belief). Charles Lightoller was one of the sailors put in charge of the lifeboats full of women and children when the *Titanic* sank. He told of his experience:

> Arriving alongside the emergency boat, someone spoke out of the darkness and said, "There are men in that boat." I jumped in, and regret to say that there actually were . . . They hopped out mighty quickly, and I encouraged them verbally, also by vigorously flourishing my revolver.

Oddie's comment:

> The sinking of the *Titanic* remains as a kind of modern icon of the assertion of sacrificial and Christ-like male authority over the female within the Christian dispensation: perhaps some of the successful and powerful male "supremacists", who died so that their wives and daughters might live, remembered as they calmly awaited death, the prayer (based on

Ephesians 5) which the parson had read at the marriage cere-
monies of many of them: "Look mercifully upon these thy servants, that both this man may love his wife, according to thy
word (as Christ did love his spouse the Church, who gave
himself for it . . .) and also that this woman may be loving
and amiable, faithful and obedient to her husband . . ." To
Charles Lightoller [the priority of women and children] over
men in such a situation seemed, quite simply, "the law of human nature".

And so it seemed to us a quite natural thing, needing no
explanation and no defense, that Daddy was in charge when
he was at home. To us, this was what masculinity meant. Of
course. We never thought about a father's "office," an office
bestowed on him by the Lord Himself, nor did we notice that
to bear that office always means sacrifice. Not until we ourselves were granted the privilege of parenthood did we learn
that a parent's authority is a *sacrificial* authority, requiring the
laying down of one's very life.

The *Te Deum,* an ancient hymn of praise, says, "When Thou
tookest upon Thee to deliver man, Thou didst humble Thyself
to be born of a Virgin. When Thou hadst overcome the sharp-
ness of death, Thou didst open the Kingdom of Heaven to all
believers." Our salvation and deliverance required the humiliation of the Savior and Deliverer. To open to us His home in
glory, He had to die. Likewise those who bear authority con-
ferred by the Lord must also humble themselves and "die"—
"Husbands, love your wives, just as Christ loved the church
and *gave himself up* for her to make her holy" (Eph. 5:25–26
NIV, italics mine).

The price of the salvation of a home and family is *sacrifice.*

❦

A man's headship over his wife is characterized not by
tyranny, cruelty, or bossism, but by sacrificial—that is, self-
denying, self-abandoning—love, Calvary love, the love that
took Jesus to the Cross. "Be imitators of God, therefore, as
dearly loved children and live a life of love, just as Christ
loved us and *gave himself up* for us as a fragrant offering and
sacrifice to God" (Eph. 5:1–2 NIV, italics mine).

Our good friend Frank Murray was nearing eighty when his wife of many years died. He had been married to his second wife just one year when he sat one morning at our breakfast table and I asked him how he understood a husband's "headship." Here was a seasoned Christian, an earnest student of the Bible, a man who exemplified godliness. I waited eagerly for his reply. He gazed at the ocean for a while as though the question had not occurred to him before. Finally, with a slow smile, he said, "Why, I don't think I've thought much about it."

"Haven't thought much about it?" I said, surprised.

"Why, no. Haven't had to. The Word is very plain, isn't it? Nothing to argue about at all."

"People are always arguing with me about it. What can I say to them?"

He thought some more.

"Protection. Headship means protection."

Then he recalled an incident when he was a newlywed the first time. A difficult decision arose. As he wrestled with it his wife, Lois, said,

"You've *got* to get it right!"

Frank knew Lois would submit to his decision, whatever it might be, therefore "getting it right" was a serious matter, much more difficult than mere arbitration, for as her God-appointed head he must protect her from a wrong decision. Perhaps it would mean sacrifice on his part—relinquishing his own preference because it would not be best for her.

"I never forgot that," he said.

I include this little story because it sounded just like what my father's response would have been, whether in relation to my mother or any other place where he held a responsible position: I've *got* to get it right.

Gerald Vann, in *The Son's Course*, writes,

All power implies a corresponding responsibility; and the greater the power the greater the responsibility because the greater the danger . . . One of the fearful things about power is that we cannot measure the effect of the abuse of it: if we wantonly hurt other human beings we know that evil will come of it but we cannot foretell the extent of the evil . . .

Because He has told us clearly that to sin against His creatures is to sin against Himself we must see all abuse of power in this light . . .

Yet the power is given us; we cannot be rid of it. Authority has to be exercised; personal gifts have to be used: how can we make sure that our use of power will not in fact be an abuse of it? Only by making ourselves powerless before God, as the dead body of Christ was powerless; only by becoming "stripped and poor and naked" within our own souls, so that the Spirit can invest us with his divine power and transform our impulses and cure our pride.

Those whom God chose to bear high authority over His people Israel, Abraham, the Father of Many Nations, and Moses, the mighty Deliverer, were called to great sacrifice— Abraham to lay his own son on an altar, and both to lay down their life's plans and offer themselves in obedience to God for the sake of God's people. Moses found the job almost too hard to bear at times, and cried out to God to release him. It does not take the fathers of ordinary families long to realize that children, no matter how sweet and how much loved, get in the way. The future looms before many a new father in a new light, with the sometimes terrifying realization that this job may very well shut out the fulfillment of cherished ambitions. How will he climb the professional ladder now with so many other demands on his time and strength? Worse yet, can he even keep chin above water, manage to bring in enough to house, clothe, and feed these small people who have such big needs? And what about . . . and what if . . . ?

A true man will certainly be brought to his knees in contrition and helplessness as he looks into the face of his newborn child, a human soul for whom he is now to answer to God. Who is sufficient for these things? An honest man knows he is not ready. Everything depends on the attitude with which he receives his burden from God—with resentment and a desire to evade it as much as possible, or with gratitude, accompanied by a frank confession of fear, reluctance, or whatever negative feelings may arise, then prayer for help to do the job right, for grace to do what he cannot do without it. He has

God's promise, "He who fears the LORD has a secure fortress, and for his children it will be a refuge" (Prov. 14:26 NIV).

❧

A family is a microcosm of the Family of God, and the same Law of Love governs both, the specifics of which are spelled out in Paul's letter to the Colossians:

Wives, submit to your husbands, as is fitting in the Lord.
Husbands, love your wives and do not be harsh with them.
Children, obey your parents in everything, for this pleases the Lord.
Fathers, do not embitter your children, or they will become discouraged (Col. 3:18–21 NIV).

Again in his letter to the Ephesians Paul gives a similar list, including a repeated warning to fathers:

Wives, submit to your husbands as to the Lord . . .
Husbands, love your wives, just as Christ loved the church . . . Husbands ought to love their wives as their own bodies.
Children, obey your parents in the Lord, for this is right.
Fathers, do not exasperate your children; instead, bring them up in the training and instruction of the Lord (Eph. 5:22, 25, 28; 6:1, 4 NIV).

The apostle Peter, inspired by the same Spirit, wrote also of the need for wives to be submissive to their husbands. He is more forceful and specific when he addresses the latter: "Husbands, . . . be considerate as you live with your wives, and treat them with respect as the weaker partner and as heirs with you of the gracious gift of life, so that nothing will hinder your prayers" (1 Pet. 3:1, 7 NIV). A man who begins to feel that his prayers are not getting through to God or not being answered might look well to the cause Peter states here.

Love means sacrifice. Each member of the family, in one way or another, has to learn to give in, give up, and give over, for the sake of the rest. When the family is planning how to spend a Saturday afternoon it is unlikely the vote will always be a unanimous one. Several will have to give in, and it is nice if they do so graciously. Love is always gracious. When somebody needs help with something, somebody else must give up what he wants to do in order to help. Somebody is having a specially hard experience. Others must learn how to put themselves in his place, how to comfort and sympathize. Doing the little things nobody thinks are *fun* but which have to be done by somebody—opportunities for self-giving and sacrifice, all of them.

A father who is bringing up his children according to God's law "puts the hay where the sheep can reach it"—teaches, for example, that it is not enough to claim that you haven't punched anybody today or run off with anybody else's toys or cookies, haven't teased your little brother or argued with your mother. He must teach positive acts of thoughtfulness such as doing obvious things without having to be asked—feed the baby his applesauce, pick up the garbage the dogs strewed around, help a younger child clean up his room, replace paper and pencil taken from the telephone by someone else. Love sees what ought to be done and does it.

A father's thoughtfulness or thoughtlessness will be reproduced in his children. Our father's gentleness and respect for Mother set the tone for us. No amount of talking penetrates as deeply as example.

A primary complaint of wives is that their husbands promise to fix things and never carry through. They begin a project and leave it half-finished. Wives tell of living without doors or light fixtures in their homes for years because their husbands begin what they call remodeling, tear things up, and get bored halfway through. Then it's time to watch the Super Bowl, and after that the home project doesn't seem important.

On Saturdays we often saw our father going around with a can of Three-in-One oil or a screwdriver, oiling squeaky hinges or tightening things. He fixed washers on the faucets and cleaned out sluggish drains. If Mother needed some job done, big or little, he was conscientiously prompt about it. I *think* my four sisters-in-law would testify that his sons have followed his example.

A man may have a reputation for kindness in the shop or office, yet be thoughtless and selfish to his wife and children. Charity must begin at home. My father's chickadee call to

Katharine Gillingham with her parents

KG, left, in her Buick

Philip E. Howard, Jr. (smallest child on rug), with his grandfather, Henry Clay Trumbull and family

PEH, Jr., center back, *with parents, brother Trumbull, sisters Anne and Alice*

PEH, Jr., and bride, June 14, 1922

Gale Cottage, Franconia, New Hampshire (KGH on porch), scene of honeymoon

KGH with Elisabeth

The Howards in Germantown, with their first four

Author's birthplace, 52 Rue Ernest Laude, Brussels

103 West Washington Lane, Germantown, Pennsylvania

3 West Maple Avenue, Moorestown

29 East Oak Avenue, Moorestown, New Jersey

Seated: *Dave and Phyllis (his wife), Elisabeth, Margaret (Phil's wife) with daughter Kay, Phil, Jim;* back row: *Tom, Ginny, Mother, Daddy, 1951*

Mother was the first sign of his arrival home. After embracing and kissing her he always greeted us with affection and good cheer. He was not one to rush to the kitchen and swing into action there—Mother did not need that. He might take up the evening paper, but he was seldom oblivious to us and our needs. If there was a sick child upstairs he went quickly to see him. For the first nine years of my life I was prone to ear-aches, tonsillitis, colds, and fevers. I loved to hear his step on the stairs, see his tall frame fill my doorway, and feel his hand on my hot forehead as he asked how I felt. I knew he felt sorry for me, and that was comfort.

Of Eliakim whom God appointed to be a father to the people of Judah it is written,

> I will lay the key of the house of David on his shoulder; what he opens no man shall shut, and what he shuts no man shall open. He shall be a seat of honour for his father's family; I will fasten him firmly in place like a peg. On him shall hang all the weight of the family, down to the lowest dregs—all the little vessels, both bowls and pots (Isa. 22:22–24 NEB).

Vivid analogies here—the man with the keys, the one in charge, steward, protector, guard. Also the peg supporting all the weight of the family. If he is not firmly established in his place, recognizing its full meaning, accepting its full burden in honor before God, the family cannot help but suffer. And pegs are not noticed for the work they do, nor are they usually thanked!

My father's sense of responsibility for his family could hardly have been stricter. It seemed at times an overwhelming burden, and he suffered under its weight. There were lessons of trust in God, of casting all his care on Him, of receiving the all-sufficient strength God promises, which took him many years to learn, even though he knew by heart the relevant Scripture passages. How often I heard him repeat the words which had been given him as a college student, grappling with the most momentous decision of his life: *My grace is sufficient for thee for my strength is made perfect in weakness.*

He knew his own weakness. He was to need a great deal of that divine strength in order to be obedient to the special command to fathers: "Bring them up in the training and instruction of the Lord."

Bring them up means much more than merely "allow them to grow." Bringing up children is a task. It is positive action. The "keys" speak of safety and protection. The "peg" speaks of firmness, strength, stability, and something not usually to the modern male's taste: staying put.

The father is the priest in the home. This means standing in the presence of God for others. It means making sacrifices on their behalf. In a deep spiritual sense he stands in the place of God in the home—His representative, the visible sign of His presence, His love, His care. A little child wants "somebody with skin on," he wants the father to be there in the dark, his weight felt sitting on his bed, his hand on the child's hand, his voice audible. His own father's arms are all he yet knows of the Everlasting Arms. As the child grows he is conscious of more than the physical presence. He watches everything the father does and tries his best to imitate it exactly. He stands by the mirror and watches him shave, puts on Daddy's shoes, jumps to place his own little feet in Daddy's footprints in the sand, lugs his briefcase, tries out his hammer or his computer, wants to sit on his lap and steer the car.

> Set an example . . . in speech, in life, in love, in faith and in purity . . . Be diligent in these matters; give yourself wholly to them, so that everyone may see your progress. Watch your life and doctrine closely. Persevere in them, because if you do, you will save both yourself and your hearers (1 Tim. 4:12, 15–16 NIV).

Those words are from a letter to a young pastor, but how perfectly they apply also to a father.

CHAPTER 19

TRUST

One cloud remains, that by thy birth
Thou enterest a ruined earth,
My little one.

But thou shalt find with sweet surprise
Earth but a pathway to the skies,
My little one.

Such is our trust, for, Lord, we give
Thy gift to Thee! O then receive
Our little one.

Receive her, Lord, and let her be
Thine own to all eternity—
Thy little one.

*T*his is the prayer of a Christian well known in the nineteenth century, H. Grattan Guinness, father of Geraldine Guinness Taylor (Mrs. Howard Taylor), author of many biographies. It expresses his own trust, and commends his child into the Lord's hands. My parents dedicated each of us to Him, recognizing their children not primarily as their offspring, much less as their possessions, but as souls entrusted to them to give back to God, confident of His power to guard and keep what they committed to His care. God chose Abraham as the Father of Many Nations, "so that he will direct his children and his household after him to keep the way of the Lord by doing what is right and just, so that the Lord will bring about for Abraham what he has promised him" (Gen. 18:19 NIV).

One of my father's favorite hymns being "How Firm a Foundation," it very early became one of my brother Dave's favorites too. I remember him as a little towheaded boy in short pants, perhaps three or four, lustily singing those great lines:

> How firm a foundation, ye saints of the Lord,
> Is laid for your faith in His excellent Word.
> What more can He say than to you He hath said,
> To you who for refuge to Jesus have fled?

God's word to Abraham was followed to the letter, though it must have seemed to the faithful father of the beloved Isaac anything but "excellent." The story tells us that this was a test.

> He said to him, "Abraham!"
> "Here I am," he replied.
> Then God said, "Take your son, your only son, Isaac, whom you love, and go to the region of Moriah. Sacrifice him there as a burnt offering on one of the mountains I will tell you about."
> Early the next morning Abraham got up and saddled his donkey.

Imagine—no discussion at all. Not even a question. The man got up early and set out to do exactly what God had said. As he took the knife to slay the boy a voice from heaven called his name: "Do not lay a hand on the boy . . . Do not do anything to him. Now I know that you fear God, because you have not withheld from me your son."

A second time the voice came, "Because you have not withheld your son, your only son, I will surely bless you" (Gen. 22 NIV).

That is faith. Abraham took God at His word, incredible as must have seemed the command, and staked everything on it.

He moved in obedience, trusting absolutely in his God to the point of raising the knife.

The establishment of a child's trust in God begins with his trust in the word of his parents. My father regarded untruth in any form as one of the "carnal weapons" which Christians ought never to use. He listed some commonly accepted forms of untruth:

exaggerated advertising;

overstatements to make an impression;

withholding certain important aspects of the truth in business transactions, lest a buyer lose interest;

cheating railroads on tickets, or customs officers on imports;

so-called "white lies" told with the false idea that good may come;

saying different things about the same matter to different people, to avoid trouble or gain advantage;

and little dishonesties which are so common in business, and which are excused because "everybody does them"—as though the multiplication of evil makes it right.

He told us the story of a boy who learned very early to trust his father's word implicitly and to obey instantly. He was playing one day on the railroad tracks. His father saw that a train was coming and had not time to rush to the boy's rescue. He called out to him to lie down at once between the rails. Without question or hesitation the boy did so. The train roared over his head, leaving him uninjured. This was a solemn lesson to us in trusting the word of our father and doing instantly what he told us to do. I wish I could say we were always instantly obedient—we weren't—but I can say with certainty that none of us ever had cause to doubt his truthfulness. Our father was truthful and conscientious almost to a fault. As Mother observed, relative to their refusal to play the Santa Claus game with us, his keen sense of honesty may have been gleaned partly from his grandfather Henry Clay Trumbull's book, *A Lie Never Justifiable.*

Ironically, perhaps, the Trumbull family (my paternal grandmother's) was noted for wild and colorful exaggeration. When Grandpa accidentally broke a teacup Grandma declared, "He simply THREW it on the floor!" When she, a small frail old lady, fell against a large bookcase she assured us she had shoved it "at least a foot." We enjoyed that trait, as did my father, I think, but he cautioned us to have a stricter regard for the truth.

When I was faced with a wrong thing I had done, I could not possibly look into the face of either my father or my mother and lie. We were expected to tell the truth, the whole truth, and nothing but the truth, and children generally live up to parents' expectations. Expect them to lie and they will lie.

When I was about seven or eight I decided to try the adventure of doing something very, *very* bad. I wanted to see how it felt to sin boldly and deliberately. I made a conscious decision to steal something, and began to seek an opportunity. As I was about to leave my friend Essie's house I saw a Mickey Mouse watch lying on a newel post. No one was looking, so I snatched it up, put it into my pocket, and started home. As I turned the corner, perhaps a hundred yards from Essie's house, I could not endure what my conscience was telling me. I raced around through the back yard and deposited the watch on the back steps, terrified of having to face Auntie Sue or even Essie, in case they had already missed it, and having to tell them the truth. So far as I know, no one ever learned how that watch traveled from the newel post to the back steps, but I do hope they found it without stepping on it.

Ours is the God of Truth. Satan is the Father of Lies. How often we see parents not only evade the truth but lie openly to their children. What could be more destructive of a child's moral fabric? Recently we saw a young mother hurrying through an airport, a baby in her arms, a pocketbook and carry-on bag over her shoulder, a screaming two-year-old in tow. As she passed us we heard her say, "You see that trash can over there? You quit that screaming, or I'll dump you into that trash can!" The awful threat had no effect. The child had learned that his mother doesn't tell him the truth. He kept screaming.

Failure to carry through when something has been forbidden may not be called lying, but when a child knows he can wheedle his parents until they give in, he is being taught— "programmed"—not to trust their word. If a child asks why about something he has no business knowing and the parents fabricate a reason instead of straightforwardly telling him he does not need an answer, they are instructing him to fabricate.

Truthfulness is the foundation of faith. My father and mother laid a sure foundation for us in the trustworthiness of their own word. If it was their *word*, it was to be trusted. If *they* said it, we knew it was true. They were not so foolish, however, as to feel they must explain everything. Often when we asked why we got "Never mind" for an answer, or "We'll see," which usually meant that when they had "seen," a no would be forthcoming. They did not think it a good thing to explain all of their reasons and actions to us when we were small. It is an unnecessary waste of time, for one thing, for the reasoning rarely satisfies the child anyway, but more importantly, it makes it difficult later on for the child to accept what God says without explanation. He must learn to trust the *person*, to believe the *word*, and to let the matter rest *there*, even when reasons are hidden, a hard but vital lesson for the rest of his life.

Because all of us are born in sin, all of us are rebellious, some more than others. Some children seem to be born sweet and compliant, others are called "strong-willed" when what they really are is merely willful--governed by will without yielding to reason, obstinate, perverse, stubborn, as my brother Phil was in his high chair when he refused to drink his milk. Mother's steadfast insistence on obedience was not for her personal victory over a "strong" will, but rather to strengthen her small son's will to enable him to will against himself, that is, to do the thing he ought to do before doing the thing he wanted to do. How many adults have remained willful, selfish, and immature because they were denied this essential lesson in childhood.

Parents must exercise mercy along with judgment. The will of the parents for small children is the law of conscience and of God. One wise father suggests that parents should give their commands in such a way that children are not forced to be transgressors of their will; and if they have already become such, they should be "disposed as much as possible to repentance." This takes more wisdom than most parents possess, but divine wisdom is promised to those who ask for it. My parents asked for it every day, I think.

There are different ways of issuing commands. A calm, matter-of-fact, and loving manner is much more likely than a stern and imperious one to inspire willingness to obey. But there are times when love is refused. Mother was certainly calm and loving in telling Phil he only needed to drink his milk before he got down. Psalm 107 is a tale of the Lord's mercy which endures forever and His people's willfulness and disobedience. He redeemed them from the hand of the foe, but they got lost in the wilderness, were hungry and thirsty, and cried to the Lord in their trouble. He delivered them from their distress, led them by a straight way, filled them with good things, but they rebelled against Him and ended up in prison and forced labor. Again He brought them "out of darkness and the deepest gloom and broke away their chains," yet some "became fools through their rebellious ways and suffered affliction because of their iniquities." They lost their appetites, nearly starved to death, cried to Him again, and again He saved them, sent forth His word, healed them, rescued them from the grave.

The story goes on—His longsuffering, His patience, His far-reaching love. At last they were humbled by oppression, calamity, and sorrow. The psalm ends with these words: "Whoever is wise, let him heed these things and consider the great love of the Lord" (NIV). What an example for parents!

CHAPTER 20

LOVE IS PATIENT AND KIND

If we could put into words our highest ideals of all that is most lovely and lovable, beautiful, tender, gracious, liberal, strong, constant, patient, unwearying, add what we can, multiply it a million times, tire out our imagination beyond it, and then say that it is nothing to what He is, that it is the weakest expression of His goodness and beauty, we shall give a poor idea of God indeed, but at least, as far as it goes, it will be true, and it will lead to trustfulness and friendship, to a right attitude of mind, as child to father, and creature to Creator. (Janet Erskine Stuart, *The Education of Catholic Girls*, p. 5)

*I*f only we could grasp what He is. If only we could remember that it is that longsuffering, mighty, Everlasting Love who chastens us, not for revenge but for a glorious reason (that we may share His holiness), perhaps we would not respond with such petulance. The love of our Heavenly Father is *patient* and *kind*. He loves us too much to want us to go our own way.

" 'My son, do not make light of the Lord's discipline, and do not lose heart when he rebukes you, because the Lord disciplines those he loves, and he punishes everyone he accepts as a son.' Endure hardship as discipline; God is treating you as sons" (Heb. 12:5–7 NIV).

There are so many wrong ideas about God. Wrong thinking about Him leads to wrong thinking about His actions. If, deep in our hearts, we bear any shade of resentment against Him for the way He has treated us, that resentment can easily be taken out on our poor little children. Failure to see divine discipline as evidence of divine love can lead to a wrong, and consequently very destructive, idea of disciplining them. God is not out to get us or get back at us. He loves us with an everlasting love. He is our Refuge when we are afraid, our Strength when we are weak, our Helper when we cannot cope. Parents stand in the place of God for their children. They must be for them refuge, strength, and helper, not adversary.

When I reached adulthood my mother told me it had not been easy for her to learn to express physically her love for us. I am not sure whether she had ever received much demonstration of love from either of her parents (I think of her father as the Grandfather Who Never Smiled—at us children, at any rate). If there was little from her parents there was less from her stepmother. So it was *not easy* for Mother, but she tried, and with the help of God she learned to do much more than came naturally to her. The babies in our family were all rocked and sung to, as I have mentioned, and there were goodnight kisses for all who were young enough to be tucked into bed at night. When we went away to school and college there were strong hugs and much effort to hold back the tears and to smile as the train pulled away. We knew we were loved and would be sorely missed. Letters, about which I will tell later, were full of love. When any of us was to perform in any public way, our parents were there. For all of this I am glad and thankful.

Parents, expressing love for their children by physical warmth and tenderness, greatly contribute to their children's later comprehension of Refuge, Strength, and Helper as attributes of God. The parents' faith in His perfect love and perfect sovereignty lays the foundation of the home in which the child is growing up. Their object for him is happiness and fulfilment, exactly what God wants for us, according to His "hidden wisdom, his secret purpose framed from the beginning *to bring us to our full glory* . . . 'Things beyond our seeing, things beyond our hearing, things beyond our imagining, all prepared by God for those who love him' " (1 Cor. 2:7, 9 NEB, italics mine).

One day when our baby Valerie was a few weeks old Jim sat down in a reclining chair and laid her on his chest, murmuring into her little ear and patting her. After a while, thinking her asleep, he fell silent, and dropped his arms to his sides, revelling in the slight weight of the tiny child on his body. She lay quiet for a moment or two, then let out a sudden lusty wail. Laughing, Jim clasped her immediately in his arms again and assured her of his presence. Not feeling his hands upon her she had, we supposed, lost the sense of "belongingness," and thought herself forsaken, when in fact she was lying as secure as ever on her father's bosom.

So it is with us. We cannot always feel the presence of our Father God, but must trust that His promise remains true: " 'Never will I leave you; never will I forsake you.' So we say with confidence, 'The Lord is my helper; I will not be afraid' " (Heb. 13:5–6 NIV).

Jesus, when He was here on earth in what MacDonald calls "the wild weather of His outlying provinces," was still "in the bosom of the Father." There was never a moment of broken fellowship. By contrast, Israel, enduring the disciplines of the wilderness—the long and arduous journeying, the snakes and scorpions, hunger and thirst, experiences at Marah and the Red Sea—felt abandoned by the God of their fathers. They could not see that all this was the necessary preliminary to the fulfilment of God's promise to lead them to the beautiful land of Canaan. They disbelieved His word, doubted His love, disobeyed His commands.

We heard these stories countless times at home, at family prayers, at the dinner table, in our beds as we were tucked in, in Sunday School and church, in the books we read and the missionary meetings and Bible conferences we attended. We heard how the Lord led those stubborn people in faithfulness, bearing with their stubbornness, forbearing and forgiving, steadily moving them in the direction He intended. His love was patient. His love was kind. We also heard about the great heroes of faith who struggled and suffered and obeyed (and sometimes disobeyed) their God.

Fathers and mothers need to know their children as well as is humanly possible. God knows His children perfectly, knows their thoughts before they think them, knows them through and through. "As a father has compassion on his children, so the LORD has compassion on those who fear him; for he knows how we are formed, he remembers that we are dust" (Ps. 103:13–14 NIV). Human fathers and mothers, on the other hand, are not omniscient. They are faced with mystery. They do not know the child or the youth or the man their baby will become, but they know that the heartbreakingly sweet little person in the crib, so perfect when asleep, bears a human nature, and as such is sinful. Children need help. God gives to fallible parents this little boy or girl, who will certainly prove to be far from perfect, to love and train and teach, to *bring up,* in the "nurture and admonition," the training and instruction, of the Lord. It's a serious assignment. There is no higher calling.

Nothing trains and teaches so powerfully as love. Love attracts, it does not coerce. If the aim of the parents is to teach their children to love God they must show their love for Him by loving each other and loving the children. "God is love. Whoever lives in love lives in God, and God in him" (1 John 4:16 NIV).

My Elliot in-laws were a highly demonstrative bunch. They went all around the room kissing everybody good night. They greeted each other with bright and cheerful good mornings and were as likely as not, just any old time, to give even an in-law a hug for no reason at all. This was a whole new direction for me. We were used to seeing our parents hug and kiss each other and the little ones in the family, but I don't remember anything of that sort happening between brothers and sisters, and I feel no deprivation because of it.

Love not only embraces. Love also punishes—and suffers more than the one punished, although no child can believe the statement "This hurts me more than it does you"—until he becomes a parent himself and learns the truth.

It is said of Adonijah, who tried to usurp the throne rightly belonging to his half-brother Solomon, that his father had never interfered with him by asking, "Why do you behave as you do?" (1 Kings 1:6 NIV). There, I believe, is one clue to

Adonijah's treachery—no questions asked by his father. My father did interfere with me on many occasions, one of them long after I had become an adult. He asked that question almost verbatim when he saw me moving in a dangerous direction. I think I was about thirty-seven, and I deeply resented his inquiry. I look back on it now with the realization that he had good reason to question me, and he did so only because he loved me. The fact that I was no longer living under his roof did not change his love or his prayers or his desire for my spiritual welfare. He had simply obeyed the biblical injunction (Gal. 6:1) to restore me gently. He died not long after that, and I wished with all my heart that I had responded with grace instead of anger.

I once heard Henry Brandt tell how one of his adult children asked, "When are you going to get off my back, Dad?" His answer was something like this: "Probably not until I die, son. I travel all over trying to influence people for good. Why should I not keep on trying to influence my own children?"

My father's example of faithful discipline greatly helped us to understand God's discipline as an expression of His great love.

We have all had human fathers who disciplined us and we respected them for it. How much more should we submit to the Father of our spirits and live! Our fathers disciplined us for a little while as they thought best; but God disciplines us for our good, that we may share in his holiness. No discipline seems pleasant at the time, but painful. Later on, however, it produces a harvest of righteousness and peace for those who have been trained by it (Heb. 12:9–11 NIV).

J. C. Ryle wrote,

We live in days when there is a mighty zeal for education in every quarter. We hear of new schools rising on all sides. We are told of new systems, and new books for the young, of every sort and description. And still for all this, the vast majority of children are manifestly *not* trained in the way they should go, for when they grow up to man's estate, they do not walk with God. (*The Duties of Parents*)

Ryle's lament, written more than a hundred years ago, describes just what we see today.

If children learned early to respect, even to stand in awe of, their parents, they would be far less likely to get into trouble by defying other authorities God places over them. There is a bumper sticker which always gives me a jolt: QUESTION AUTHORITY. There is a place for that sometimes, if the question does not spring from a fundamental hatred of authority but is an honest and forthright inquiry. Let us remember that as Christians "we are receiving a kingdom that cannot be shaken. Let us be thankful, and so worship God acceptably with reverence and awe, for our 'God is a consuming fire' " (Heb. 12:28–29 NIV).

CHAPTER 21

RULES

The foundation stones on which the discipline of a Christian home is laid are the three things we have been considering in the last three chapters: sacrificial authority, trust, and love. Because parents bear this sacrificial authority, because they carry the responsibility of their children's trust, and because they love God and love their children for His sake, they must establish rules or, as modern parlance prefers, "guidelines."

In many of England's tiny back gardens one sees espaliers —trees or shrubs which have been trained flat against a wall giving a two-dimensional effect. While this is drastically contrary to the direction they would have grown if left to themselves, they take up little space and produce beautiful flowers or fruit.

As the gardener who espaliers the tree cooperates with God, so parents cooperate with Him in training children in the way they *should* go, not in the way they would naturally go. Jesus used the metaphor of the vine to teach about our union with Him, a union meant to result in our bearing fruit which will glorify God.

"My Father is the gardener. He cuts off every branch in me that bears no fruit, while every branch that does bear fruit he prunes so that it will be even more fruitful" (John 15:1–2 NIV).

It is difficult to resist the pressures of our "have it your way" society, and even earnest Christian parents sometimes feel uncertain about the wisdom of drawing up so much as the briefest list of rules. Won't it make children rebel? Isn't it legalistic? What if we can't enforce them?

In our fear that we squeeze children into our own mould, we are in danger of allowing the world to squeeze us into its mould—something Paul sternly warned the Roman Christians to watch out for. God bestows on parents a very great trust. They are in charge of the "vineyard" which is the family. We may look upon rules laid down for children as the stakes and ties which keep the vine from rank growth and enable it to produce the best fruit, while the pruning might represent the parents' chastening. Jesus says, "If a man remains in me and I in him, he will bear much fruit; apart from me you can do nothing." This "remaining" is not a vague feeling of religiosity. Jesus makes it clear that it means obedience. Union with Him is impossible without harmony with His will. "Why do you call me Lord," Jesus asked, "and do not the things that I say?"

The gardener loves his garden, knows each flower and shrub and tree, understands its special qualities and needs, and gives it tender care. Parents are given the delicate task of training an imperfect and highly impressionable child who is not their "property" but is entrusted to them for a time, that they may curb the natural tendencies which are useless or destructive, and guide him instead to God. Grattan Guinness's prayer for his daughter, quoted in Chapter 19, acknowledges God's claim on her.

None of us can do a perfect job, but we may look for help to those whom God has given us as models. Here is a description of how one who had the spiritual care of many younger women mothered them:

> Being to those under her, as far as in her lay, what Our Lord was to His disciples, reproducing His humility, His charity, His goodness, His sweetness, His patience . . . never surprised at defects and imperfections . . . forming by example rather than by precept . . . leading to God . . . by love and confidence rather than by fear . . . proportioning her teaching and trials to the character, strength, and measure of grace of

each individual, making them understand that only by renunciation and death to self can they reach the goal, and ever helping them by all the means that unwearied charity could suggest. (Maud Monahan, *The Life and Letters of Janet Erskine Stuart*, p. 74)

God in His mercy told His people what to do and what not to do. My parents made rules for us, "stakes" and "ties" to help us live a peaceful and fruitful life. The keeping of these rules was our early training in that renunciation and death to self which will never be easy for any of us so long as we live in this mortal body, yet that very renunciation is the route to freedom and fulfilment. The obedient child is the happiest child.

Rules and the consequences of infringing them instilled in us a healthy fear, not only of our parents but of authority in general. My friend Essie and I, on our way to school, once trespassed on the property of a Catholic school. I have never forgotten how I shook with fear when a nun scolded us. I think it was the first time anyone other than my parents corrected me. I never set foot on that territory again. Although the Bible has much to say about the *fear* of the Lord, Christian teaching on it is rare today. Objections are raised as soon as it is mentioned. Isn't fear a base motive? Why should we fear Him who loves us as He does? If He is our Shepherd, Savior, and Friend, how can we be afraid of Him? "He is not a tame lion," as C. S. Lewis says. When Moses had given the ten commandments there were thunder and lightning, the sound of a trumpet, and the mountain was filled with smoke. The people of Israel trembled with fear, stood at a distance, and begged Moses to do the talking rather than let God speak to them, lest they die. Note the language of Moses' reply.

"*Do not be afraid.* God has come to test you, so that the *fear* of God will be with you to keep you from sinning" (Exod. 20:20 NIV, italics mine). Do not be afraid—*so that the fear of God will be with you*! The words seem oddly contradictory, but I think there are two kinds of fear here—fear of physical harm, which Moses assures them is not called for, and the fear without which they would certainly come to spiritual disaster. A child's fear of physical punishment leads him to obedience, but so does his natural desire to please the people he loves. It is the beginning of respect. Until we love perfectly, which will not happen on this fallen planet, we must fear. Until perfect love casts it out, fear is a salutary thing. Fear saves us.

The fear of the Lord, according to Proverbs, is to hate evil. It is the "fruit of humility," the "first step to wisdom," the "fountain of life." It "prolongs a man's days" and makes him "a refuge for his sons" (Prov. 8:13; 22:4; 9:10; 14:27; 10:27; 14:26 NEB).

The New Testament teaches the necessity of this fear if we want to live a holy life.

> We must all have our lives laid open before the tribunal of Christ, where each must receive what is due to him for his conduct in the body, good or bad. With this fear of the Lord before our eyes we address our appeal to men. To God our lives lie open (2 Cor. 5:10–11 NEB).

> If you say "our Father" to the One who judges every man impartially on the record of his deeds, you must stand in awe of him while you live out your time on earth (1 Pet. 1:17 NEB).

> Let us serve God with thankfulness in the ways which please him, but always with reverence and holy fear. For it is perfectly true that our God is a burning fire (Heb. 12:28–29 PHILLIPS).

Ancient writers saw the fear of the Lord as conducive to inner health; it is a lamp in a dark place, it illuminates and teaches, consumes malice, burns wrong thoughts.

George MacDonald wrote, "The fear of God will cause a man to flee, not from Him, but from himself; not from Him but to Him, the Father of himself, in terror lest he should do Him wrong or his neighbor wrong" (*Unspoken Sermons*, p. 30).

❧

I saw a film showing how a mother polar bear trained her cubs. They came stumbling out of their cave in the ice, all three of them a bit bleary from the long hibernation, the cubs dazzled by the sunshine, drunk with the freedom of the wide world spread out before them. The mother had serious business to attend to, to teach her children how to survive in a frozen world. There was no time for nonsense. She nudged them into line, showing them where to go, rolling down a snowbank (they followed fearlessly), avoiding the cracks in the ice (they jumped over them), taking them to where she could teach them to find food. Example was everything—or I should say almost everything. Verbal precepts were not needed, but a few swift cuffs to their little furry behinds certainly helped. So our loving Shepherd *leads* us in paths of righteousness, using His rod from time to time for correction and His staff for protection, both of which the psalmist found *comforting*.

In all the daily routines at home we were taught *This is what we do, This is how we do it, This is where things go*. Most of these were routines and habits established simply by the way in which our parents had ordered their own lives. We learned by watching. But what if our parents had not been there? What if we had seen more of some other "care-giver" than we saw of Daddy and Mother? The power of influence would have been diluted. "Quality time" can never substitute for ordinary days spent doing ordinary things together.

As for *what* we were to do, morning routines were firmly fixed on weekdays:

Get up.

Dress.

Eat breakfast.

Join family prayers.

Brush teeth.

Make bed.

Get ready for school.

How we did these things called for many more reminders and repeated precepts, for example:

Get up *promptly* when called.

Dress *quickly* (no meditation exercises in the middle of the floor), *properly* (we had clothes for school, play, and church, and very few for each, so we had to wear the right ones).

Come to breakfast *punctually* (at 7:10, not 7:11).

Come *cheerfully*. If anyone in our house appeared wearing a scowl he might be asked to go back upstairs and "find a cheerful face." What a death to self that demanded! What a renunciation of one's nasty feelings! I remember it well. It was not a capricious requirement. The book of Proverbs supports it: "A happy heart makes the face cheerful," "A cheerful look brings joy to the heart" (Prov. 15:13, 30 NIV), and this is more for the sake of others than for one's own.

Eat *politely*. Table manners cannot be skipped over, for if there's one area where the spiritual and emotional climate of a home is revealed it's at the table. To my parents, politeness meant, among other things:

If you can't say something nice about the food don't say anything.

Napkin in lap, everybody.

Sonny, elbows off the table.

Sit up straight, Bets. You're slouching. That's better!

Eat what is put before you.

Pass the milk to somebody else before helping yourself.

Don't reach, Davy, ask. Good boy.

Don't interrupt.

Ginny, hold your spoon properly—*like this*, not like that.

Don't make a gangplank with your knife, Tommy.

Jim, we don't eat with our knives. You have a fork—let's see if you can hold it properly. Good for you!

Don't chew with your mouth open.

Don't talk with your mouth full!

The endless repetition of these reminders can wear out the hardiest fathers and mothers and make them wonder whether it really matters *how* we go about ingesting our necessary daily sustenance. Well, more about that in the chapter on courtesy. There *was* conversation at our meals. It wasn't all rules and corrections, not by a long shot. But conversation is made more pleasant when people are behaving themselves in a civilized fashion.

❦

Being told what to do and how to do it is not all children need. They need *help* in the performance. God does not leave us to ourselves. Having told us what to do and how, He helps His children in all kinds of ways. Moses named his son Eliezer, which means "My God is my helper." God is a Very

Present Help in trouble. "The LORD is with me; I will not be afraid. What can man do to me? The LORD is with me; he is my helper," wrote the psalmist (Ps. 118:6–7 NIV), and in the prophetic writings Christ Himself speaks, "The Lord GOD will help me; therefore shall I not be confounded" (Isa. 50:7 AV).

"The Spirit helps us in our weakness. We do not know what we ought to pray for, but the Spirit himself intercedes for us with groans that words cannot express" (Rom. 8:26 NIV). "We may receive mercy and find grace to help us in our time of need" (Heb. 4:16 NIV). In his letter to the Ephesians the apostle Paul describes our helplessness when we were following

> the spirit who is now at work in those who are disobedient
> . . . gratifying the cravings of our sinful nature and following
> its desires and thoughts . . . But because of his great love for
> us, God, who is rich in mercy, made us alive with Christ even
> when we were dead in transgressions—it is by grace you have
> been saved (Eph. 2:2–5 NIV).

Grace did for us what we could not do for ourselves. And so parents, says my sister-in-law Lovelace Howard, do for their children what they cannot do by themselves, in order that they may learn to do what they *must* do by themselves.

We learned the *how* of toothbrushing by our parents doing it for us when teeth first came in, and by their helping us learn to do for ourselves. *Thoroughly* was the word. *Daily. Faithfully.* And how about bedmaking? *Smoothly.*

I have already described how carefully we were trained in where things go—a place for everything, everything in its place. There was security in this routine and consistency. Life is simplified when you know what, how, where. A hook for the car keys and the car keys always on the hook eliminate frantic scrambles all over the house with everybody shouting at everybody else about who had them last.

The ordering of a peaceful home is not possible without the application of eternal principles. It is, after all, mostly *little, common* things that make up our lives. *This* is the raw material for the spiritual life. If we despise small things, regard normal household duties as burdens, routines as boring, rules too confining, we will never learn, nor can we teach our children, to live a life of holy harmony. This takes faithfulness in the troublesome details first of all, learning to do them well that we may make of them an offering to the Lord, for it is His work, after all, given to us. It is our daily bread for which we should learn to be thankful. Such faithfulness is the groundwork for all God may ever ask us to do.

Self-preoccupation, self-broodings, self-interest, self-love— these are the reasons we jar each other. Turn your eyes off yourself; look up and out! There are your brothers and sisters; they have needs that you can aid. Listen for their confidences; keep your heart wide open to their calls, and your hands alert for their service. Learn to give and not to take; to drown your own hungry wants in the happiness of lending yourself to fulfil the interests of those nearest or dearest. Look up and out, from this narrow, cabined self of yours . . . you will find to your own glad surprise the secret of the meekness and gentleness of Jesus, and the fruits of the Spirit will all bud and blossom from out of your life. (*Joy and Strength,* p. 160)

CHAPTER 22

ENFORCEMENT: A MISSION FOR REDEMPTION

I have tried to show that the rules and regulations of the home my parents established, the order that characterized that home, and the response of us children were based on love for God. Human love is subject to many vicissitudes. My parents wisely sought to follow, in shaping our behavior, the way God deals with the children He loves.

"If his sons forsake my law and do not follow my statutes, if they violate my decrees and fail to keep my commands, I will punish their sin with the rod, their iniquity with flogging; but I will not take my love from him, nor will I ever betray my faithfulness" (Ps. 89:30 33 NIV).

We find in these words the Lord's stern demand for obedience hand-in-hand with the assurance of His changeless love. Punishment and love are far from incompatible. It is not difficult to see why the two things necessarily go together. The father who loves his son desires his growth in wisdom and grace and is therefore willing to correct him, even with a rod if need be. There are times when we cannot or will not understand why God should punish, even though we do not have difficulty seeing the necessity of the enforcement of family rules and of civil law for the good of all. Singapore is one of the cleanest, most efficiently managed, and drug-free cities in the world. Stamped across the entry visas in large red letters are these words: DEATH PENALTY FOR DRUG DEALING. It works. It not only saves the city for the citizens, but it saves many a one who would be tempted by the money to deal in drugs. His life is worth more to him than money. The law then, clearly stated and consistently enforced, is his salvation. The city itself is also saved from much crime.

"When the sentence for a crime is not quickly carried out, the hearts of the people are filled with schemes to do wrong. Although a wicked man commits a hundred crimes and still lives a long time, I know that it will go better with God-fearing men who are reverent before God" (Eccles. 8:11–12 NIV).

God is love. His will is love. His law is His love. His love is His law. It is a grossly distorted view of God Himself and of His love that finds the idea of His chastening us intolerable. Can we forget that He took our punishment on Himself before the foundation of the world? He was the Lamb slain. He loved us then. He loved us enough to pay the death penalty. Shall He love us less now? Those who come to God come to a Consuming Fire. We easily forget that, looking for an indulgent grandfather whose love, a mere sentiment, capitulates to our whims and overlooks our selfishness. God will not do that, for to do so would be to damn us. He is not willing that any be damned.

The Consuming Fire must do His work—burning, purging, refining—for His object is our perfection. How could His love want less than that? This is a far cry from the idea of mere retribution or "getting even."

A book about the shaping of our family must include the highly controversial subject of spanking. Mother's article, "Teaching Your Toddler," presented in Introduction, makes it clear that obedience must be taught. Phil, the willful little boy in the high chair, understood perfectly well that he must drink his milk. He did not want to. Mother was determined that he should. Her determination sprang from her love—she wanted Phil's best. Here were two good things: it was good for him to drink his milk, and it was even better for him to learn to obey his mother. The sound of the dogcart overcame his desire to win the argument, and he obeyed, making a spanking unnecessary that time.

"A spanking," wrote my father,

> not done in anger, will clear up a sullen attitude on the part of a young child as a thunderstorm freshens the air on a sultry day. It gets results faster than argument, is a warning to the other children looking on, and even the whipped child, deep down in his heart, realizes that he got what he deserved and is therefore quieter, more tractable, and really happier afterwards.
>
> How foolish and dangerous it is to discard the wisdom of the ages that is given us in the Bible! Said Solomon: "The rod and reproof give wisdom: but a child left to himself bringeth his mother to shame . . . Correct thy son, and he shall give thee rest; yea, he shall give delight unto thy soul" (Proverbs 29:15, 17); "Chasten thy son while there is hope, and let not thy soul spare for his crying" (19:18); "Withhold not correction from the child: for if thou beatest him with the rod, he shall not die. Thou shalt beat him with the rod, and shalt deliver his soul from hell" (23:13, 14).
>
> It is literally true that a corrected child "shall give thee rest." Right after the punishment he will stop fretting, nagging, and pulling at his mother's skirt; and when the correction is kept up through the years, along Scriptural lines, he will indeed "give delight unto thy soul." (New Every Morning, p. 92)

I remember Mother's saying to one or the other of us, "I think you're tuning up for a spanking." It was probably said to Dave more than any other. He had a mischievous streak and many original ideas on how to "get Mother's goat." She would correct him verbally, the tension would build, Dave would be more and more un-get-along-with-able, "tuning up," as it were. A spanking restored harmony.

Both Daddy and Mother were careful to see that they had our attention when giving instructions. It is both useless and unfair to issue commands to a child when you have not got his attention. Who has not seen the impatient father yelling at a child who appears to be deaf to his voice? Very likely the child is used to being yelled at (we weren't!) and knows that many delays are possible before force will be used.

Our parents called us by name. When we heard our names spoken, we listened.

Our parents looked us straight in the eye. Eye contact held our attention.

Our parents' commands were given in a normal speaking voice. One mother told me her children paid specially close attention when she spoke in a specially quiet voice. This, they knew, was serious.

If we heard the name, saw the look in the eye, listened to the word, and *then* did not budge, Mother resorted to what she called "the speedy application of a switch to little legs." This switch was a thin stick about eighteen inches long, one of which she kept over the door in every room in the house. We knew it was handy, but because we knew our parents meant exactly what they said the first time they said it, it did not often take more than the raising of Mother's eyes to the lintel to galvanize us to action. The common but very bad habits of repeating commands and raising the voice not only exhaust the parent's patience so that he then punishes in anger, but also teach the child that he need not pay attention until he has heard the command many times, and heard it shouted. Examples are all around us of children who pay practically no attention at all.

Our parents sometimes said to us that "delayed obedience is disobedience." This was a general rule, for usually when they asked us to do something they expected it done quickly. It was not a hard and fast rule. Mother was wise in that earliest lesson with Phil. There was no particular urgency about the milk's being drunk immediately. The child's desire was to get out of the high chair. So long as he refused to drink the milk, just so long must he do what he did not want to do: stay where he was. When something he desperately wanted to do —see the dogcart—came up, he had to make a terrible choice: drink the milk, or miss the dogcart.

A spanking is not child abuse. It is a deliberate measure of pain, delivered calmly, lovingly, and with self-control, on a loved child in order to deliver him from self-will and ultimate self-destruction. This is how God treats sons. My parents took their cues from Him.

J. C. Ryle says,

Punish seldom, but really and in good earnest,—frequent and slight punishment is a wretched system indeed. As to the best way of punishing a child, no general rule can be laid down. The characters of children are so exceedingly different, that what would be a severe punishment to one child, would be no punishment at all to another. I only beg to enter my decided protest against the modern [1888!] notion that no child ought ever to be whipped. Doubtless some parents use bodily correction far too much, and far too violently; but many others, I fear, use it too little. (*The Duties of Parents*, p. 27)

It was our parents' object to break the child's will without breaking the child's spirit. The difference is an important one. My friend Karen O'Keefe, who has worked with horses all her life, assures me that a horse that has been broken may be a highly spirited horse. The breaking is the bringing him under the control of bridle and rein, which are at the will of his rider. If he was lively, vigorous, and full of life before he was broken, he will continue to be. The most highly trained horses in the world, Karen says, are the Lippizaner stallions of Vienna, who are trained to do *on command* what they would naturally have done in the field. The results of that rigorous training are beautiful to behold.

The child whose will is trained to subjection is a freer, happier child, much pleasanter company than he whose own will is his only law. Those who object to the "breaking" idea may prefer my great-grandfather's choice of words. He speaks of will-training rather than will-breaking: "A broken will is worth as much in its sphere as a broken bow; just that and no more . . . Every child ought to be trained to conform his will to the demands of duty; but that is bending his will, not breaking it" (Henry Clay Trumbull, *Hints on Child Training*, p. 19).

When a little boy stolidly refuses to finish his milk he brings on himself as well as his mother real misery. The battle of the two wills cannot bring freedom and happiness to either. One must win, one give in. Under God, parents have one set of duties—to train; children have another—to obey. Both must bend or conform their wills to the demands of their position. God's word is: "Children, obey your parents in the

Lord, for this is right. 'Honor your father and mother' . . . Fathers, do not exasperate your children; instead, bring them up in the training and instruction of the Lord" (Eph. 6:1–2, 4 NIV). The child in the high chair learned a great spiritual truth: the liberty of obedience. Down he jumped and out he ran to the milkwagon. I am sure that it has been much easier for us to understand God's ways than it must be for those whose childhood was not governed by wise Christian parents.

❦

"What if God does not want me to have what I need at this moment?"

"If He does not want you to have something *you* value, it is to give you instead something *He* values."

"And if I do not want what He has to give me?"

"If you are not willing that God should have His way with you, then, in the name of God, be miserable—until your misery drive you to the arms of the Father."

"Oh, but this is only about a mundane matter. I *do* trust him in spiritual matters."

"*Everything* is an affair of the spirit. If God has a way of dealing with you in your life, it is the only way. Every little thing in which you would have your *own* way has a mission for your redemption. And he will treat you as a willful little child until you take your Father's way for your own." (George MacDonald, *Unspoken Sermons*)

"A mission for your redemption." This is how Christian parents see their enforcement of the principles on which their home is based. The child has many wants. If he sees the moon as a cookie he wants the moon. The baby learning to crawl has to touch everything, for everything holds interest for him. The toys he is given lose interest when he is capable of reaching the corner of the tablecloth and the knobs on the stove. The other side of the street looks more inviting than his own front yard, and the machine his big brother built with Legos nicer than the pulltoy Granny gave him. Why suck on the bottle of apple juice if there is a bottle of ammonia he can reach under the sink? He does not know what will destroy him. His parents do. Their refusal is his redemption.

In our home the first commands which held a mission for our redemption were *No* and *Come*. We had no trouble understanding these two words long before we were old enough to say them. Understanding was one thing. Enforcement helped us to obey.

Mother would often take a baby out of the high chair when she had finished eating and hold him on her lap at the table, a rather dangerous place to be, within reach of things he was not allowed to have. A spoon or a silver napkin ring he could play with. A glass of water he was not to touch. When the napkin ring lost its appeal he reached for the glass. Mother said no and pulled the little hand away. If he reached for it again, the word was repeated and the hand smacked. If a third lesson was needed, the smack would be harder, or perhaps Daddy would come around the table and speak sternly.

"Jimmy, *no*. You must not touch that."

My parents always presented a united front in matters of discipline. We knew we could not "play them off" against each other.

This beginning lesson was taught before we learned to crawl. Thus many agonies were eliminated. The next lesson in Mother's book, begun as soon as we began to crawl, was to teach us to come when called. She was careful to draw the child's attention first by speaking his name. She looked him in the eye. She said *come*. There might be a few seconds' pause as the child sized up her seriousness. The big blue eyes locked hers. He heard. He understood. Could he get away with disobeying? It's worth a try. Most children try. It was hard to challenge Mother. She was quiet. She was firm. All of us learned very quickly that she meant what she said. Some of us were more determined than others to disarm her. I was one of those. When she spanked me I often refused to cry. I wasn't as smart as Dave who would start to bellow and squall with the first whack and therefore received fewer than I did.

As our personalities developed our parents did their best to know and understand us, and to suit the punishments to the individual. If Mother were here to defend herself I am sure she would say she had no theories, no psychology, and not nearly enough understanding of her children's differing temperaments. When people asked for her "secrets of success" she would laugh and say she never had any. She loved her children, and she prayed and tried to go by the Bible, as did Ruth Graham, who kept an open Bible and a hickory stick on the kitchen counter.

Far more material is available today to help parents appreciate the differences between their children and to proportion training according to their strengths and weaknesses. There is so much emphasis on child psychology, in fact, that it is possible to be greatly intimidated and greatly confused. Some young couples are so terrified of the complicated responsibilities of parenthood that they opt not to have children at all. I believe that trust in God, love for one's children, and prayer for wisdom are a recipe for successful parenthood far more reliable than all the books and seminars in the world.

"Each child can be trained in the way *he* should go, but not every child can be trained to go in the same way. Each child can be trained to the highest and fullest exercise of *his* powers, but no child can be trained to the exercise of powers which are not his" (Henry Clay Trumbull, *Hints on Child Training,* p. 9).

❦

Some parents are too lenient, some too strict. Many err on both sides. I have told how my father was too hard on my oldest brother, and asked his forgiveness in later years. "Do not embitter your children," the Bible says, "or they will become discouraged" (Col. 3:21 NIV). No new father is an expert when he receives his firstborn. God knows that. He gives children to people who are brand-new at the job and have to begin at once to do things right. They do a lot of things wrong, but God in His mercy rights many of the wrongs and hears the prayers of the humble who ask His forgiveness and His help. God heard my father's prayers for help to be more understanding, more gentle, more tender.

We learned to tell the truth—first by the example of our parents. Honesty was no mere policy. It was an unequivocal standard of righteousness, never broken by our parents. We could absolutely depend on their word. What they said they would do they did. It is a cruel thing when parents break

promises to little children. We had to keep our promises too.
If we accepted an invitation to a party we went to the party,
no matter how exciting an alternative might later be pro-
posed. Only the most dire necessity warranted cancelling a
music lesson.

If we were naughty Mother could usually read it in our
faces. One of my brothers had a habit of sidling into the room
and saying very sweetly, "Hello, Mommie!" which was the
signal that his activities needed to be investigated. If she
faced us with a misdeed we did not dare to lie about it. The
punishment was to have our mouths washed out with soap. I
don't remember suffering that more than once. The memory
is vivid—being taken firmly in hand and led to the laundry
shed, a great bar of yellow soap rubbed on a washcloth, and
the inside of my mouth vigorously scrubbed, Mother im-
pressing upon me all the while how great an evil was lying.

Integrity, reliability, steadiness, thoroughness were con-
cepts not talked about but demonstrated by the life lived before us. These are what may be called the "harder" virtues,
developed through small renunciations and sacrifices, building the principles of self-discipline without which life is
hardly worth living.

Respect for elders was strongly enforced. I remember a
hard spanking, given over my mother's knee with a hair-
brush, because I spoke disrespectfully to old Mr. Stevenson
next door. The pain of the spanking was not worse than having Mother say, "Betty Howard, I'm *ashamed* of you."

Respect for private property was another lesson. When
Tom was about four he waded into the Richies' newly cleaned
fishpond next door and deliberately churned everything up.
For this he was debarred from the privilege, very rare for any
of us in a given summer, of going to Virginia Lake to swim.

When I was in the third or fourth grade the whole class
began pounding on desks once when the teacher left the
room. Of course she heard us far down the hall. When she
came back she asked who had been pounding. I had to tell
the truth. So humiliated that I dared not look around, I raised
my hand. Whether it was the only hand raised I do not know,
but I will never forget the shame I felt when she pointed to

me and said, *"You!* Of all people!" That was enough punishment for me.

We learned the habit of sitting still—in the car, at the table, at prayers, in church. Wriggling could result in our being sent to our rooms or made to sit on a chair for a specified time, even occasionally sent to bed. Sometimes the car had to be stopped when a spanking was needed.

To some readers I am sure the vigilance of my parents will seem oppressive. It does not seem so to me as I look back. There may have been nervousness and anxiety in it at times. I'm sure there was, given the temperaments of both mother and father. But vigilance is necessary, and with God's help parents can avoid the sort that "rouses to mischief the sporting instinct of children and stings the rebellious to revolt," as Janet Erskine Stuart says, and they can exercise

> the vigilance which, open and confident itself, gives confidence, nurtures fearlessness, and brings a steady pressure to be at one's best. Vigilance over children is no insult to their honor, it is rather the right of their royalty, for they are of the blood royal of Christianity, and deserve the guard of honor which for the sake of their royalty does not lose sight of them. *(The Education of Catholic Girls,* p. 42)

CHAPTER 23

ENCOURAGEMENT

*I*n all of us there is strong resistance to a forced obedience. Even in an infant we see the stiffened back, the defiant expression. But gentleness, patience, tenderness, and encouragement bring out the best in us.

J. C. Ryle writes,

> We are like young horses in the hand of a breaker: handle them kindly, and make much of them, and by and by you may guide them with thread; use them roughly and violently, and it will be many a month before you get the mastery of them at all. Now children's minds are cast in much the same mold as our own. Sternness and severity of manner chill them and throw them back. It shuts up their hearts, and you will weary yourself to find the door . . . You must set before your children their duty,—command, threaten, punish, reason,—but if affection be wanting in your treatment, your labor will be all in vain. (*The Duties of Parents*, p. 4)

A careful reading of the apostle Paul's letters to the young churches under his care will discover the affection of a true father-heart. He could be stern, as he was to the Corinthians, correcting them about divisions in the church, about exalting one man above another, worldly immaturity ("I could not address you as spiritual but as worldly—mere infants in Christ"), boasting, arrogance, sexual immorality, lawsuits among believers ("Why not rather be wronged? Why not rather be cheated?"), arguments about what to eat and what not to eat, even cases of gluttony and drunkenness at the communion table. One gets the impression that that first-century church was in a real mess, almost as bad as some in this century. Yet it was still a church with sanctified members. Paul begins his letter, "To the church of God in Corinth, to those sanctified in Christ Jesus and called to be holy, together with all those everywhere who call on the name of our Lord Jesus Christ—their Lord and ours" (NIV). The awful condition of the church did not make it no church. Paul was determined to do all he could by the power of God to help them to fulfil their calling.

Called to be holy. If fathers of families could keep ever before their eyes this single high purpose toward which they seek to guide their children, what a difference it might make in the homes of our nation! And how shall they guide them unless they themselves are holy? This must be their constant prayer: *For their sakes I sanctify myself.* The greatest need of families is holy parents.

And how shall parents *bless* their children? Among the many meanings of this word *bless* are "to pray for the happiness of" and to "make happy, blithesome, and joyous." How should we do this? Showering children with material things is often the first thing modern parents and grandparents think of to make them happy. When I think of what made me happiest as a child it is not the tangible gifts I received, even though these meant more to me than such things can possibly mean to many present-day children because they have so many. I think of the pleasure my parents and grandparents showed in me. They never lavished compliments on us (I don't think we would have been ruined if they had parted with a few more!), but we treasured any least word of encouragement. Bringing home a report card with all *A*'s was a great happiness for me, even though it was more or less expected, and children generally live up to expectations. When we did that we knew our parents were pleased. Mother smiled, although she was not given to waxing very eloquent. Daddy always said, "That's *fine*." Those words were prize enough for me. Our performance was not the result of relentless goading, or even the prospect of great rewards, but of that "steady pressure to be at our best," to do what was *right*. Realizing how unbelievable some of this may sound to readers, I checked my memory with my brothers. They agree that this is the way it was. *Why* was it? Example is by far the best answer. It was the way our parents lived. The consistency of what we saw, the dependability of their word, the clarity of their requirements backed up the example.

The apostle blesses his spiritual children with grace and peace from God our Father and the Lord Jesus Christ, and goes on to thank God for them and to recount the ways in which His grace is increasingly being manifested in them. They have all the spiritual gifts they need, he says, and reminds them that Christ will keep them strong to the end, for He is faithful. His hopefulness must have given them great impetus to correct their ways.

It is important to choose the right time, the right place, and the right tone when correction is needed. Suppose children misbehave when they are away from home? Is that the right time and place for correction? Children watch for the weak spots on the battle lines. If they find they can get away with things in the grocery store, in the car, or at Granny's house, they will certainly avail themselves of the opportunities. While it is necessary sometimes to punish a child in the presence of his siblings, for convenience' sake and in order that the siblings may learn from example, I think it is unfair and unwise to embarrass him in front of those outside the immediate family. Because we knew our parents would not tolerate behavior elsewhere that they would not tolerate at home we did not often put them to the test. When we dared to do so, however, a stern look and a quiet reprimand were usually all that was needed to subdue us.

The right tone is exceedingly important. I knew a young mother who habitually shrieked at her children, even if all was well and she only wanted to ask one of them to close the door. She seemed to have no other form of address to them but a shriek. Not surprisingly, the children all shrieked too. The place was pandemonium all the time. On the only occasion when I ever tried to carry on a conversation with her she shrieked at the children to be quiet. When there wasn't the least reduction of noise she laughed and said to me, "Look at that! They don't even HEAR me!" Poor children. How could they?

Paul's tone in his letter to the Thessalonians is one of great appreciation, sympathy, and compassion. He begins with grace and peace to them, and thanksgiving to God for them. He calls them "brothers loved by God." He commends them for having received the Holy Spirit's message in spite of their severe suffering, and tells them they have been a model to other believers. His motive was not popularity.

> We were not looking for praise from men, not from you or anyone else. As apostles of Christ we could have been a burden to you, but we were gentle among you, like a mother caring for her little children . . . You know that we dealt with each of you as a father deals with his own children, encouraging, comforting and urging you to live lives worthy of God, who calls you into his kingdom and glory (1 Thess. 2:6–7, 11–12 NIV).

What little child is not thrilled to show his father something he has done to please him? One of the things Mother gave me to do when I was sick in bed was making scrapbooks. I would cut up the old *Saturday Evening Post*s (I especially loved the Campbell Soup Kids advertisements) and paste pictures which I could hardly wait to show Daddy when he came home. If I learned a new piece on the piano, I wanted to play it for Daddy. When I wrote a book many years later, I waited more eagerly for his response than for any other's. "My, Betsy, this book is an *achievement*!" he said of one of them. It was not his style to be effusive—ever. But we knew when he was pleased, and we treasured his least word of encouragement. He was interested. He was attentive. I heard recently of a father who, when his little girl snuggled up next to him on the sofa, got up and went to sit in a chair. When I hear such a story, I think of Malachi's prophecy—Elijah "will turn the hearts of the fathers to their children, and the hearts of the children to their fathers; or else I will come and strike the land with a curse."

My father's heart was turned to his children. He was not only an encourager but also a comforter. I sometimes had nightmares and would call out in fear. The hall light went on. My bedroom door opened, and I could see the tall silhouette of my father in his old wrapper. "What is it, Betsy?" He sat down on the bed and took my hand. He sang hymns—"Safe in the Arms of Jesus," "What a Friend We Have in Jesus"— and often gave me a Scripture verse for a "little pillow" to go to sleep on, such as "He careth for you," or "Lo, I am with you always." His presence brought God's presence to my bedside.

Besides encouraging and comforting, my father urged us in every way he could to live lives worthy of God. To my brother Jim, who was experiencing a tough testing in a matter of the heart, he wrote,

> I am so pleased at the way you and ——— handled the affair, putting the Lord first and trusting Him . . . I am always thankful when I hear that any of my children have faced trial in the strength of the Lord and with the "comfort of the Scriptures" (Romans 15:4). If you become saturated with the Bible, you will always be able to find some comfort and strength in every situation in life. I have read it systematically for forty-four years, and am finding today that the Lord continually brings to mind the things from it I need to meet the temptations and problems of life. I am on my twenty-eighth trip through the Bible this year [he was sixty-three], making notes as I feel led . . . I pray for you usually four times a day.

He was keenly aware of the example he had to set not only for us but for those who looked to him as an authority because he was editor of a much-read Christian magazine. His exposure there brought him plenty of criticism, which he sought to receive graciously. "Always look for the grain of truth in every criticism" was his rule. He tried to learn whatever God might be wanting to teach him, remembering the word in Proverbs, "My son, do not despise the LORD's discipline and do not resent his rebuke." A rebuke from a reader which would naturally provoke resentment might be a rebuke from God Himself, who dares to give pain when needed for the sake of greater good. Conversations at the dinner table about some of these criticisms led to his explaining that if we learned at home to accept the corrections of our parents who loved us, we would not have so much difficulty in accepting criticism from others.

God knows the feelings of discouragement, inadequacy, and failure which conscientious parents feel. But it was *His* idea to make them parents and to give them this particular set of children. He knew they would not do a perfect job. He is Father to the parents, and promises every kind of help they need. He stands beside them in every situation, ready to give wisdom as needed and grace to help in time of need if only they will turn to Him and ask for it. He teaches them (see 1 Cor. 13) how to love these children:

Love is patient. Love is kind. It is not easily angered. It keeps no record of wrongs. It always protects, always trusts, always hopes, always perseveres. Love never gives up.

It is a supernatural love. It is beyond our powers to love in this way, but it is not beyond His. Amy Carmichael's prayer sprang from her experience of mothering hundreds of Indian children:

> Give me the love that leads the way,
> The faith that nothing can dismay,
> The hope no disappointments tire,
> The passion that will burn like fire.
> Let me not sink to be a clod—
> Make me Thy fuel, Flame of God.
> (*Toward Jerusalem*, p. 94)

CHAPTER 24

FRANCONIA

The life lived and the things loved are what form a child's character and tastes. It would be impossible to exaggerate the importance to our family of Gale Cottage in Franconia, New Hampshire. *Cottage* is not the word one would choose nowadays, but in the nineteenth century any house where people spent the summer was a cottage. All along the coast of New England there are huge houses built at that time, all with servants' quarters and many bedrooms, nevertheless called cottages. Our cottage was not huge, and its style nothing like Cape Cod's. It was what we would now call a lodge, built entirely of wood, inside and out, with no plaster anywhere. There was no cellar. The house rested on (was not fastened to) granite rocks. There were two large rooms downstairs which we called the living room and the "pahlah" (mimicking the New England pronunciation of parlor), two large and two small upstairs, and two servants' rooms in the attic.

Mother tells of her first visit there at the end of the summer of 1921. Her fiancé Phil Howard had come from Camp Allagash on Moosehead Lake in Maine, where he had been a counsellor, to the Gillingham cottage on Lake Cochnewagan in Monmouth, Maine, bringing an unusual gift to his beloved —a beautiful ashwood canoe paddle made by one of the guides at the camp and inscribed with PH on one side and KG on the other.

Mother takes up the story:

٨ We had some wonderful canoe rides on the lake and when it was time for us to leave my father had agreed to drive back to Germantown via Franconia. From the garden we took a huge bag of fresh corn with us for the Howards which was greatly enjoyed for dinner that night at Gale Cottage, the big table having been carried from the porch into the living room and placed in front of the fire, which I thought such a good, though somewhat novel, idea.

Once my father was headed home there was no stopping him, so bright and early the next morning we started off. It was not a sad parting for Phil and me since we could look forward to lots of happy visits all the next year and to our honeymoon at the Cottage the following June.

Elsewhere I have told of the famous HAM we ate in all its forms on our honeymoon, but I don't think I told *how* it was cooked. There was no kitchen in those days. A small woodshed contained a two-burner kerosene stove. It was not the most ideal arrangement, but honeymooners are not too particular about such things and we had a glorious two weeks in the place I came to love even more than I had loved Monmouth.

Then what about the summers when we were there with our children? Betty has told [in *All That Was Ever Ours*] of what the Cottage meant to a small child and then to a mature person. I can't possibly say it as well as she has. I can, however, make a few comments from the point of view of the mother.

"I'll just stick around the good old Cottage" has become a family quote as I used that phrase so often over the years. Plans would be afoot to climb up to Lonesome Lake, or strike out for the Falling Waters Trail on Lafayette, or perhaps the fishermen of the family would think they might find "greener pastures" for fishing (how's that for mixing metaphors?) by a seventy-five mile trip northeast to Lake Umbagog, the source of the

beautiful and trout-filled (they hoped!) Androscoggin
River! A few times I got to go along but in the earlier
years there was often a small tot who would soon tire of
such a trip so I was happy and content to "stick around
the good old Cottage," and said so quite firmly. I might
add that on several occasions the fishermen drove up the
drive after dark and Dad would make a circle of his
thumb and forefinger to indicate the success of their
efforts. I would then suggest they try a few holes in Gale
River or Pond Brook and almost without fail they would
sheepishly return with several small but nice trout!

In the early days when Phil, Betty, and Dave were very
small, facilities for washing clothes posed a problem. A
kitchen had been built by then but there was only one
way to wash clothes and diapers. No laundromat was
even heard of then. Three big blue enamel pails served for
wash tubs, two big kettles heated the water on the
kerosene stove. As for cleaning the big place—I used to
say that if Aunt Annie Slosson had had to clean it herself
it would have been built very differently—but aren't we
glad she didn't? There is just no place to compare with it
in the minds of most of us, I'm sure.

What those mountains meant in the lives of each one of
our six cannot be imagined! They prepared Phil for many
a trek out into the bush with his Indians. Betty had no
problem in hiking into Aucaland, over rough terrain and
wading through rivers. Dave surmounted the mountains
of Colombia on more than one occasion, Ginny found it
easy to push through rough trails to see her missionary
friends in the heart of Palawan [Philippines], Tom broke
records going up and down Mt. Washington in a matter of
hours, and Jim snowshoes over the northern Minnesota
landscape with no effort at all.

They all learned at least to "doggy paddle" in the hole
by the big rock in Gale River, a good start to become the
swimmers they all are now.

For patience and precision there is nothing better than
learning to fly fish in the icy waters of the mountain
streams, and these lessons were taught Dave and Jim by
their skillful father. Creeping down Black Brook, pushing

their way through the thick alders with small rods and a short line, usually resulted in a nice creel full of beautiful dark native brook trout.

In the evening, as the mist slowly formed on the meadows, and the haunting song of the white throats vied with the bell-like tones of the veery and the hermit thrush, and the purple light faded from the sides of Lafayette, there was a longing in one's heart to just *keep* things that way always! But this joy could not stay with us, as there was another added joy as we turned into the big Cottage living room and a huge fire was lit in the lovely fireplace. These memories cannot be taken away from us, and as Amy Carmichael says, "All that was ever ours is ours forever!" ல

In 1975, when the Cottage had become a burden too great to be borne by our Aunt Anne Howard who owned it at that time, it was to go on the market. We all grieved. That the scene of such gloriously happy family times was to pass into the hands of people who could never love it as we did was almost unbearable. For love it we did—every spruce block and shingle of the house itself, every room, every piece of furniture, the antique pitchers, basins, bowls, and clock; the mountains spread out to the south, the pine woods to the west, every shining rock of the cold brook. It was to go to strangers. But Isak Dinesen said that one can bear anything if one can put it in a story. So I wrote about it in *All That Was Ever Ours*:

It was to me as the very vestibule of heaven. We would leave Philadelphia on the night Pullman, the "Bar Harbor Express," and I remember the delirium of joy with which I settled into the berth, my clothes safely stowed in the little hammock, and fell asleep, to be awakened in New Haven by the shifting of the cars as the train was divided into different sections. I would lift the blind and see the brakeman passing with his lantern, watch the baggage trucks rolling by, and try to read in the dim light the thrillingly romantic names on the freight cars in the yards —"Seaboard Airline," "Lackawanna," "Chicago and North-western," "Route of the Phoebe Snow," "Atchison, Topeka, and Santa Fe." I remember the jerking of the uncoupling and the satisfying crunch of the coupling, the loud hissing of steam and then the gentle rolling out of the station, the giant engine building up speed until the *clickety-click* reached the rhythm that once again put me to sleep.

In the morning I woke to see the Connecticut River valley, and it was not long before we pulled into Littleton, were met by my grandfather's Buick and driven the eight miles to the Cottage. My stomach tightened with the joy of that first glimpse of the two brick chimneys, visible as we crossed the Gale River Bridge, and then, as we turned up the driveway, I could see the beloved house, the breakfast table set in the sun on the front quarter of the porch. (The porch ran all the way around the house, which was rectangular, built stockade-style, with six-inch spruce blocks for walls in the lower portion, shingles above.)

The sound of footsteps hurrying from the kitchen on the old boards. The creak of the hinges on the massive door which had a key eight inches long. (It was said that Uncle Will had the big iron lock and key before he built the house, and had to construct a door to fit the scale.) A race around the porch to see if the little cart we played with was still in its place, to look into the separate cabin which was the kitchen at the back of the porch, a pause to look at the mountains—Lafayette, Artists' Bluff, Bald, Cannon, Kinsman—blue against the sky, always dependably the same, strong, comforting ("So the Lord is round about them that fear Him"), waiting for us to climb them once more. In the living room, the huge fireplace with its three-foot andirons; the green china clock on the mantel, the guns in their niche; the fishing rods cradled in bentwood hooks suspended from the ceiling; the Texas Longhorns, the moose antlers, the deer head; the portrait of Uncle Will on the walls; the rocking chairs where Grandpa and Grandma Howard always sat by the heavy writing table which Uncle Will had made with his own hands; the converted kerosene lamps; the little melodeon which was used for accompaniment at our Sunday evening hymn sings (the "natives" came to these, including a little old lady who claimed she couldn't sing "half's good's a crow"); the cushioned settee with a lid which lifted to reveal a furry mechanical bear, a black lace parasol, a music box, and a mummified human child's foot, brought from some ancient tomb in Egypt by Uncle Will when he was scrounging the world for things to put in the then new Metropolitan Museum in New York.

In the back parlor were crumbling leather-bound books, a set of bells, a stereopticon with magic pictures of ice caves and frozen waterfalls, astonishing in the perfection and depth of each gleaming crystal, the glass cases of moths and butterflies which Aunt Annie had lured by stretching a bedsheet in the light of a lantern on the porch at night. And upstairs were books and more books, brightly colored stuffed birds from foreign lands, Aunt Annie's flower press, a vial of attar of roses from a forgotten tomb, and life-sized paintings of improbably large brook trout that Uncle Will had caught, painted, and pasted to the door panels. There was the little room with the bird's-eye maple furniture where I slept, snuggling down under a feather quilt and listening to the wind in the white pines, the sound of the river flowing over the stones, and there was a poem tacked to the wall, "Sleep sweetly in this quiet room, O thou, whoe'er thou art . . ."

And oh, the smell of the place! Year after year it was the same. Year after year we rushed in and breathed that sweetness—old wood, old leather, old books, the perfume of pine and balsam and wood smoke. There is no accounting for that fragrance, but it is still there, still the same, intoxicating to us who know it, still redolent of all the years of happiness, and now someone else will breathe it, someone who doesn't know its meaning at all.

Well, there was a reprieve. It was rented by many people for some years and then bought not by strangers but by members of the fourth generation to follow Uncle Will and Aunt Annie.

❦

To be removed annually from Washington Lane's hot macadam and carbon monoxide pollution to the cool freshness of the White Mountains was God's gift to our family. Uncle Will and Aunt Annie, who were childless, could not have dreamed when they built that unique house in 1889 that they were instruments in divine hands for the blessing of a large family so many years later.

It seems to me of supreme importance for parents to try to arrange, I would almost say at any cost, some sort of getaway place for their family. To be physically removed from the scenes of ordinary life and routine is refreshment that cannot be found in any other way. Our family life was never governed by the radio, so we did not need a respite from that. Perhaps families today need, more desperately than they realize, to put distance between themselves and the telephone and television set, at least for a specified time. Quietness, open space, time are essentials for re creation.

Nature itself furnished most of the amusement we loved in Franconia. Evenings by the fire, reading (*books*, not newspapers or magazines, not in Gale Cottage), or playing "Go Bang" or charades furnished the rest. There were no forms of entertainment that cost money or shut us away from simple pleasures. Often I would go alone into the field to sit in the sunshine with my thoughts, hidden from view by the tall, warm, fragrant grass, or down the path in the woods to the Meeting of the Waters, as Aunt Annie had named the joining of Pond Brook and Gale River.

There was a real attic where we found a little leather stagecoach trunk with a curved lid. Aunt Anne (niece of Aunt Annie) or somebody had taped a sign to the top of it which said, "Why, here they are, right here in this little trunk!" And there they were—toys.

Gale Cottage afforded us the opportunity to study art—of a sort. There were ancient woodcuts depicting Adam and Eve confronting Satan, or angels and cherubim and stallions and obese ladies in impossible positions. These had been relegated to the dark recesses of the eaves, probably by Mother, because, hanging over our beds, they gave some of us nightmares—so she said. I suspected it was because most of them portrayed one or more beings, celestial or terrestrial, who in her opinion were not adequately clothed. These my brothers and I crawled into the dusty dark to study at our leisure.

I had time to study zoology—little creatures I could not have gotten to know without lots of time. The tiny brown field mice with delicate pink feet which ran up and down the electric wires and scattered seeds among the picture frames and mattresses of the attic were my friends. I would lie on my stomach holding my breath, not moving an eyelash, waiting for them to appear at their holes in the floorboards. Another friend was a little chipmunk who had a hole near the back porch. We would put crackers for him on the step and watch him from a distance as he tore up to seize them and raced back to the hole. That wasn't good enough for me, however. I wanted to look him in the eye. I waited until I was sure he was in the hole, sprinkled cracker crumbs and peanuts around it, and lay down with my nose about two feet away. After what seemed forever up would come the tiny snout, down it would go in a flash. Over and over and over. I never moved, never made a sound. At last his longing for those peanuts was too strong for his fear. The beady eyes looked into mine. One day I succeeded in coaxing him to eat from my hand.

We studied botany. Aunt Anne taught me the names of the flowers that grew near the Cottage, and together we pressed them into a brown dime-store notebook—cinquefoil, Quaker lady, and twin flower from the pine woods, wild orchid and lady's slipper from the low, grassy place at the river's level, devil's paintbrush, butter-and-eggs, goldenrod, and Queen Anne's lace from the sunfilled meadow. Years later I learned the bracken, ferns, and mosses, and showed other small children the wonders of the hairy cap moss, how you can take off its hairy cap, lift the lid of the tiny "salt shaker," and pour out its pale green powder into the palm of your hand.

Tom describes the botany lessons our father gave us on a mountain-climb:

> In the first half-hour or so, when you were still walking along under the hardwood trees, he would point out the bunch-berries, clintonia borealis (there seemed to be no English name for this plant with the long single stalk and one shiny, dark blue berry), and moose maple. He told us that the enormous moose maple leaves would always serve as a useful substitute if you had forgotten to bring along tissues in your pack.
>
> Further up you began to see Labrador tea and creeping snowberry next to the trail, and the hardwoods gave way gradually to spruce trees. A few tall straight ones would appear among the birches and maples; then the hardwoods disappeared and on either side of the path there would be dense growth of scrubby, gnarled spruces, their immemorial roots grasping the moss-covered rocks like tough old fingers that had been holding on against winds and blizzards since the

beginning of the world. My father would take out his penknife and cut off little deposits of spruce gum that had oozed through the lichen-covered bark and give them to us to chew. You felt that this was a much cleaner and healthier confection than Wrigley's or Dentyne. It was certainly more astringent and less sugary.

As the trail climbed higher the trees grew stubbier and stubbier, until suddenly you found yourself at the timber line. Often a single step would take you from the scrubby spruce growth out into the immense upland above the timber line, with the whole world spreading away from you.

. . . The song of the white-throated sparrows came like a crystal echo up from the spruce forest below . . . My father would call back and forth to them, and would stop every few minutes just to sniff the air and gaze, with his hands on his hips. On most trips he would observe at least once that the scene here was a very long way from Thirteenth and Wood, the dingy corner in Philadelphia where his office was. (*Heroes*, p. 309)

And so we children were shaped. It is said that we are transformed in what we love. We thank God for giving us His mountains, forests, and streams to love, and that beautiful place Uncle Will had no idea he was building for us.

CHAPTER 25

WORK
AND
PLAY

"*I* commend the enjoyment of life," says the Teacher in Ecclesiastes, "because nothing is better for a man under the sun than to eat and drink and be glad. Then joy will accompany him in his work all the days of the life God has given him under the sun" (Eccles. 8:15 NIV).

Work should always be associated with joy. Being on vacation did not exempt us from work. Wherever we were there was a balance of work and play. Mother and Dad were never exempt from work—why should we be? We were all members of the family. Everybody but the baby was a *working* member of the family. The worry of some parents, that by requiring work they would be depriving their children of childhood, never crossed our parents' minds. They would have been amused, I suppose, if anyone had suggested such an idea. Doesn't everybody know that play is more fun if interspersed with work? And how shall we ever learn to work if we don't begin in childhood? My father believed that when God ordained hard work for man after he sinned, God knew that his wandering thoughts and imagination would need to be kept in check and his mischievous hands would need to be kept busy. If there were no need to earn money, each man would be a law unto himself, and we would soon have chaos instead of the large measure of order that we do have.

Mother's share of the housework, the lion's share always, was much more difficult in Franconia than it was at home, but I was not aware of that until I was trying to do the work she did there. The frying pans were too thin, and the saucepans were bent and would not sit firmly on a burner. The kerosene stove was too small and was given to smoking. The only oven was a cumbersome tin one which had to be set over the burners, putting them out of use for anything else. There were no cabinets in the kitchen, only open shelves. The sink had only one faucet, the drainboard was made of wood, counterspace was nearly nonexistent. There was an icebox, not a refrigerator, and it had to sit on the porch because it wouldn't fit into the kitchen. It had a drip pan underneath which had to be emptied. The garbage went into a pail suspended on a hook to foil the thieving raccoons. To us this was all fun. To Mother it was work, but she took it cheerfully.

The story is told of three women washing clothes. A passerby asked each what she was doing.

"Washing clothes" was the first answer.

"A bit of household drudgery" was the second.

"I'm mothering three young children who some day will fill important and useful spheres in life, and wash-day is a part of my grand task in caring for these souls who shall live forever" was the third.

I am reminded of Amy Carmichael's story of a donor to her work in Dohnavur, South India. He wrote that he wanted his money to go into "spiritual work." In her experience in India, she said, she found that souls were "more or less firmly attached to bodies." Bodies require houses and therefore housecleaning; food and therefore cooking; clothes and therefore washing. Amy, who had spent years in itinerant evangelism, was willing to relinquish that for motherwork, and became *Amma* (Tamil for "Mother") to many hundreds of Indian children. "I wonder how many thousands of tiny fingernails and toenails I have cut!" she said.

Ordinary work, which is what most of us do most of the time, is ordained by God every bit as much as is the extraordinary. *All* work done for God is *spiritual* work and therefore not merely a duty but a holy privilege. When Moses brought the people of Israel together to transmit the Lord's commands concerning the tabernacle he said,

> Each of you set aside a contribution to the LORD . . . gold, silver, copper; violet, purple, and scarlet yarn; fine linen and goats' hair; tanned rams' skins, porpoise-hides, and acacia-wood; oil for the lamp, perfume for the anointing oil and for the fragrant incense . . . Let every craftsman among you come and make everything the LORD has commanded.

They came, "men and woman alike came . . . every Israelite man and woman who was minded to bring offerings to the LORD for all the work which he had commanded through Moses did so freely" (Exod. 35:5–10, 22, 29 NEB).

When Solomon built his temple there were lumbermen, carpenters, and stonemasons, goldsmiths, silversmiths, and workers in bronze. There was also that remarkable man Huram who could do anything—"an experienced worker in gold and silver, copper and iron, stone and wood, as well as in purple, violet, and crimson yarn, and in fine linen; he is also a trained engraver who will be able to work . . . to any design submitted to him." Solomon had seventy thousand hauliers and eighty thousand quarrymen, among other workmen. All had a share in the stupendous labor of building the house of the Lord.

What a difference it might have made in the way we did our work if we had clearly understood that our house was also the house of the Lord. While the habit of work had been so strongly established that we hardly gave a thought to making our own beds, cleaning our rooms, washing and drying dishes, setting the table and helping with the laundry, emptying the "scrap baskets" (a New Englandism my father clung to) and burning the rubbish—those were all routine—I'm afraid I did complain about having to sweep the big Cottage living room with a pushbroom. This meant taking up a number of throw rugs, carrying them outside and shaking them, sweeping the wide wooden staircase, and moving a lot of furniture. It was a *chore*.

At the Cottage we enjoyed most of the jobs which were different from those at home—carrying wood from the woodshed to the fireplace, running down to the icy little spring in the grove with an aluminum pitcher which we carried, frosty and dripping, back to the dinner table, walking to the post office for our mail in the days before home delivery, going across the field to Mr. Smith's barn and watching while he and Mrs. Smith poured the foaming pails of milk into the hand-cranked separator. We brought the milk home in glass bottles with cardboard tops. There was always a small bottle of thick yellow cream and occasionally some of Mrs. Smith's cottage cheese which we mixed into a delicious farrago with strawberry jam. I don't remember hearing the boys complain about having to dig worms in the manure pile or cut brush from the trail in the woods or clean the ashes and lay the fire in the fireplace. I loved cleaning the spring, and I loved polishing things—oil lamps and chimneys, brass candlesticks, the fender in the parlor fireplace. I also loved rummaging through cupboards and the closet under the stairs—"snooping," Mother called it, but my snooping was rewarded one day when I found a new pair of glasses, still in the mailing case, which my grandfather had been looking for, for years.

It went without saying that we must refrain from the things we most enjoyed until we had finished the things we did not enjoy. "No dessert until you finish your spinach" was the principle—sweep the living room before you go swimming.

My parents' understanding of work would, I suppose, be called "the Protestant work ethic," but surely it's older than that. The Bible opens with God working. The proportion was six days of work to one day of rest, a formula that has never been improved upon. Children sometimes need to hear the command, "Six days shalt thou labor and do all thy work," with the emphasis on the word all. When work is faithfully, thoroughly, and conscientiously done from Monday through Saturday, Sunday can be relished. Through high school and college, although away from home, I was thought rather peculiar because I kept the family rule of no studying on Sundays. This meant that I had to do all my schoolwork in the previous six days. How I looked forward to listening to the symphony in my college room and luxuriating in an afternoon nap while everybody else was trying to make up for a weekend busy with affairs other than academic. I was open to the charge of legalism, of course, but I saw it as a declaration of freedom: on this one day in seven I am free to rest.

God gave Adam work to do. Angels work, and so, surely, do the saints in glory. The biblical picture of heaven is not one of lounging on clouds—"His servants shall serve Him" is what it says. Jesus worked hard when He was here on earth. The sin of Sodom was idleness—"pride, fullness of bread, and abundance of idleness" is the Authorized Version. The New International Version has "arrogant, overfed and unconcerned."

"Idleness is the devil's best friend. It is the surest way to give him an opportunity of doing us harm. An idle mind is like an open door, and if Satan does not enter in himself by it, it is certain he will throw in something to raise bad thoughts in our souls" (J. C. Ryle, *The Duties of Parents,* p. 22).

My father lived by the verse he had given the boys at Stony Brook School: "Study to be quiet, and to do your own business, and to work with your own hands." Knowing that he must answer to God for his children he saw to it that there wasn't time for us to hang around the drug store or the street corners where idlers congregated. Young people today don't hang around, I'm told, but I do marvel at the amount of time they seem to have to hang *out.*

My brother Dave, the most (perhaps the only) really enterprising one of the six of us, went out and got himself a paper route, only to be told sadly by his boss that he was too young. Not wanting to lose the good route, Mother insisted his older brother Phil take it on for a couple of years. Phil was not terribly pleased, preferring rather to watch birds or trains. Delivering those papers no matter what the weather, no matter how many birds and trains he had to miss, was good medicine, strengthening him against himself by checking impulse and teaching the priority of duty, lessons without which no man ever goes very far. Tom also was a paper boy, but had such a bad time keeping accounts that he claimed he paid *The Evening Bulletin* for the privilege of delivering the papers.

One of my father's favorite authors was Horatius Bonar. Now and then we would hear a quotation from this worthy, such as:

Let us "redeem the time." Desultory working, fitful planning, irregular reading, ill-assorted hours, perfunctory or un-
punctual execution of business, hurry and bustle, loitering and
unreadiness,—these, and such like, are the things which take
out the whole pith and power from life, which hinder holiness,
and which eat like a canker into our moral being.

In 1943 Mother came down with a serious case of undulant
fever. We three older ones were all away at school, so Ginny,
who was nine, was given a chance to mature a little faster
than she would have, a chance to give *herself*. She shouldered
the responsibility of getting up early enough to fix breakfast
for Daddy, Tom, and Jim. She took trays upstairs to Mother
and Nana, and before going off to school washed the dishes
while Tommy dried them. If anyone had suggested that this
was too great a load for a little girl to bear, she would have
been the first to deny it. The joy of serving, of feeling herself
indispensable to the family, was her reward.

❦

And then there was play. We knew how to amuse ourselves. Every afternoon when we came home from school we
played outdoors. In Germantown the yard was very small,
but we spent hours "playing cars," which meant constructing
roads in the dirt, building tunnels and bridges, and running
toy cars over them, complete with sound effects, of course.
    We had sleds which we used on our little bank in front of
the house, or on the McCallum Street hill which was just
around the corner. On Saturdays Daddy would take us to
sled on "Tommy's Hill," in Fairmount Park, a marvelous
slope which swooped down into a sort of bowl where we
could zoom around and down across the frozen Wissahickon.
It meant a long climb back up through the woods, but it was
worth it.
    Something called a sled-wagon, a sled on wheels, was in-
vented in the thirties. Everybody had one. My brothers would
make trains of these with the neighborhood boys, lying on
their stomachs and hooking their toes into the bumper of the
one behind. It was a dangerous business, speeding down Mc-
Callum Street. Once the boys put me on the tail end of such a

train, and as they whipped around the corner at the bottom of the hill I was flung off the wagon and shot into the middle of the street, scraping chin, elbows, and knees. I don't think I boarded that train again.

There were forty-two boys in our neighborhood and two girls besides me. One of the girls was not often permitted to play with me because we went to the wrong church. The other one moved away when we were both in the second grade. My friend Essie lived many blocks away, so chances to play with her were rare. We played house on her porch, turning over the rocking chairs and draping them with blankets, making beds for our dolls inside and using Essie's long-suffering cat for a fur around our necks or a pillow for ourselves when it was "bedtime." We spent hours at this, going through all the motions of cooking, eating, housekeeping, child-tending. Nothing was as much fun to me as creating little "cozy" places where my nesting and ordering instincts came into full play. We hollowed out a wonderful hiding place in the vacant lot behind Essie's house, clearing out all the brush and stacking it vertically to make walls, tamping the earth till it was smooth as a floor, and sweeping it clean. In the corner of my bedroom we moved two bureaus to make two walls, tucked our dolls cozily into their beds, and set their tiny tea table.

Then there was Monopoly. When Monopoly came in everything else went—or so it seemed to me, for Dave and Phil would disappear to Buddy Stiles's porch and spend whole summer days. As usual, to the boys' activities I was not invited.

Both in Germantown and in Moorestown, the whole neighborhood seemed to choose our yard to play in, no doubt because our parents encouraged it. Some of our friends were not allowed to bring friends home. We could bring anybody anytime—our parents would rather have us nearby and know who our friends were and what we were up to. Kick the Can was a variation of Hide and Seek which we played often after school when we moved to Moorestown, racing around the house, into the bushes, and through the hedge into the Richies' or Huntingtons' yards.

Across the street was a florist business with a row of greenhouses. They discarded very large wooden boxes which we were allowed to take. We built houses with them, houses which we called "bunks," stacking the boxes, making a roof with boards, and covering the doorway with old rugs. I can even remember building a fire and cooking something, sitting in the doorway. I felt wonderfully cozy and peaceful in our little house. I haven't heard for a long time of children playing games like this. They must always be *going* somewhere, to participate in organized recreation which requires elaborate equipment, supervised by adults. Surely they can't be having as much fun as we had, and I feel sorry for them! I recently overheard a little girl insisting that she must be transported somewhere to play basketball because she "couldn't get any exercise" otherwise. The mother, foreseeing the long-term car problems this would lead to, refused. When the child protested loudly, the mother's calm reply was "You are perfectly capable of riding your bicycle or taking a walk."

There was a limit to our playtime as to everything else. We had an hour or so in the afternoon before piano practice or paper route time. Theophan says,

> One should have in view that in strengthening the powers of the body one should not thereby inflate self-will and destroy the spirit for the sake of the flesh. To avoid this the chief things are moderation, a definite schedule, and supervision. Let the child play, but let it be in the place and in the way which are indicated to him. (*Raising Them Right*, p. 34)

Compared to the immense piles of toys many children accumulate today, our toys were very few. There were several reasons—far fewer were manufactured. We hadn't money to spend on many toys. Our parents did not believe happiness lay in the possession of *things*. People did not shower us with gifts.

Mother often noted that small children tired quickly of most toys, but could occupy themselves endlessly with pots and pans, measuring cups and spoons, or a bucket of soapy water on the back steps. When Tommy was two or three he loved to take out the paper bags from the drawer where she kept them and spread them across the kitchen floor. This was permitted on one condition: that he put them back when he finished playing. One day Mother found the bags all over the floor, but Tommy was in the living room where Daddy was playing the piano. She went in and told him to put away the bags. With a smile of seraphic sweetness he looked up at her and said, "But I want to sing 'Jesus Loves Me'!" Here was an occasion to teach the great principle that obedience is better than sacrifice. It's no good praising the Lord when you're being disobedient to your mother.

Following a talk in which I had described the discipline of our family a man said to me, "Wow, am I glad I'm not your brother!" I asked what he meant. "I could never have survived that rigid discipline! I don't like to be too regimented. I like to have fun."

Ours was not a family with Pickwickian stories of outrageous scenes, pratfalls, slapstick. I search my memory in vain for anything of that nature. But oh, we had fun. We *did* have fun! I don't know any family that knows how to laugh harder than the Howards. We don't just giggle, titter, or chuckle. We guffaw. We belly laugh. We shout and scream and subside into wheezings and gasps. Dad's minutely accurate descriptions of situations and people often broke us up at the dinner table. When he would read to us from Henry A. Shute's *Real Diary of a Real Boy* we would get to laughing so hard he couldn't go on. Mother, Tom, and I would be wiping the tears of laughter. Ginny's eyes would close, and she would throw back her head. Phil, Dave, and Jim would be writhing in their chairs, grabbing their knees and rocking back and forth as though in pain.

Hilarity we had plenty of, and still do. Whenever we get together we not only love to sing the old hymns (*Tabernacle Hymns* No. 3), but we always include several rounds of charades. Either of these can go on for hours, the latter sending us to the point of apoplexy with laughter when it's Tom's turn. He's irrepressible as actor and mimic, and so far we have never succeeded in stumping him with anything, be it book title, song, poem, or slogan.

In trying to get at just what it was that struck the Howard funny bone, Tom and Lovelace analyzed it as *words,* always something to do with words—books, word games, the *bon mot*, different ethnic or geographical accents, expressions or pronunciations, mimicry.

Phil is a born mimic, able to imitate not only any foreign accent but the sounds of a steam train pulling into and out of the station—sounds so accurate we felt we were there. Tom used to make faces which actually looked like the front grilles of cars. We could tell (in those days before all cars began to look alike) whether he was doing a Buick, Ford, or Cadillac. He loved hats and headdresses, and could twist a bath towel around his head in a half-dozen ways.

We had so many family bywords which to this day fill our conversation that it is quite impossible for an outsider to understand what in the world we are talking about. The in-laws in self-defence have had to learn them all.

Tom's Sunday school class furnished us with some good ones. Trying to quiet the boys for the lesson the teacher had said, "Let's have a word of prayer." One boy who did not simmer down received a sharp jab in the ribs from another who said in a loud voice, "Let's have a word of *prayer*, Winston!" Once when asked to read the story of Jesus calming the sea a boy read, "The wind ceased and there was a dead clam." Another, instead of reading, "The Lord reigneth," read "The Lord resigneth." When "Stinky" (yes, that was what everyone called him, poor little boy), listening to the story of Saul's anointing as king, heard the phrase, "they filled the horn with oil," he imagined a different sort of horn. Fluttering his fingers as though on the keys of a brass instrument, he tootled familiar bars from The William Tell Overture: "Too-too-*toot*, too-too-*toot*, too-too-*toot-toot-toot*, BLOOP, BLOOP, BLOO-OOP!"

Phonograph records were another source of quotes. Into our conversations we throw lines from Ruth Draper's "The Italian Lesson," from the English record of "Beyond the Fringe," which includes a Welsh miner who wanted to be a judge, and from Joyce Grenfell's "The Nursery School," or "Shirl's Girlfriend."

Nobody could have had more fun than the Howard family. Our live entertainment was better than any big screen.

CHAPTER 26

COURTESY

*L*ittle Jim puts down his spoon and begins the slow, careful climb down from his high chair.

"Thank you, Mama," he says in his southern accent. "Ah en*joyed* that!"

What a lovely thing that was for this grandmother to hear! How unusual in our times—courtesy from a small child who had not been prompted. He had picked up what he heard from his elders. The power of example again. So often what is picked up is quite the opposite—the flung-down spoon, the rush from the table with nary a thought for the meal or the one who prepared it.

Courtesy is plain old-fashioned thoughtfulness—what will make the other person most comfortable? Do for him or her what you would want done for you. Nobody is born thoughtful. We must all learn it.

Oswald Chambers wrote, "Yield in childhood to selfishness and you will find it the most enchaining tyranny on earth" (*My Utmost for His Highest*, p. 74).

To parents is given the holy task of teaching their children *not* to yield to selfishness but to learn the mystery of charity, which means self-giving, sacrificial love. This is a profound concept, the groundwork for which is the elementary lesson that the world does not revolve around *me*. It is not too soon to begin this lesson on the baby's first day at home. This may seem ridiculous to new parents, but how much chaos and agony may be averted if the wisdom of experience is heeded. My parents didn't think it was too early, nor did Gladys West Hendrick who wrote that wonderful little handbook *My First 300 Babies* (obtainable from Windsor Publications, 335 Laurel Ave., Arcadia CA 91006, telephone [818] 358-7557). She was a midwife who often stayed with the new mother for several weeks after delivery, helping her and the rest of the family to learn practical procedures of baby care and training "so that all parents may experience the real joy of parenthood: assurance in caring for their little ones, freedom from uncertainty, and freedom from the anxiety that often accompanies the addition of a new little member into the home. This is the basis for a child's security and future development." So Mrs. Hendrick writes in her introduction.

Her philosophy is summarized thus: "It is not what the baby does—for at times he would seem unpredictable—it is what you do about it."

Her authority is unexceptionable, having been gained not only through being a mother and grandmother herself, but in having helped (at the time she wrote the book) over three hundred babies make their debut into the world, and having handled each individual case by the same routine. *Each* individual case by the *same* routine? But isn't everybody "special"? we ask. "There have been *no* exceptions," she says.

My mother believed in giving a baby a routine which I took to be the right way until my own baby arrived. Then I decided Mother's method was outmoded and a bit too strict. I was up two and sometimes three times a night feeding Valerie, taking my cues from the Indians who were my only neighbors. They knew nothing but on-demand feeding which made perfectly good sense to me, although it was more difficult for me to carry out than it was for them. Their babies slept in the bed or hammock with them. They had no schedules for anything, no deadlines, no work that required heavy concentration. When my daughter's babies came she had been well indoctrinated with La Leche League's humanistic philosophy of on-demand feeding. When her sixth child was born she was given a copy of *My First 300 Babies*. She says it changed her life. It worked—much better than La Leche's casual program.

Henry Clay Trumbull says that the Hebrew word translated "train" in the Bible occurs only twice in the Old Testament and has no equivalent in the New. Those who were brought up in the household of Abraham, "the father of the faithful," are said to have been "trained" (Gen. 14:14). A proverb emphasizes a parent's duty to "train up" his child with wise consideration (Prov. 22:6). Nowhere else in the inspired record does the original of this word "train," in any of its forms, appear. Its origin seems to have been in the habit, still prevalent among primitive peoples, of opening the throat of a newborn babe by the anointing of it with blood, or with saliva, or with some sacred liquid, as a means of giving the child a start in life by the help of another's life. The idea of the Hebrew word thus used seems to be that, as this opening of the gullet of a child at its very birth is essential to the habituating of the child to breathe and to swallow correctly, so the right training of a child in all proper habits of life is to begin at the child's very birth.

Mrs. Hendrick gives very simple and specific rules for that first day home from the hospital, beginning with the welcome home—the eager relatives and well-meaning friends, the clicking cameras and the father's inspection. All this will probably be over by 11:30 A.M. when it's time for a nap. The mother needs a rest too by now, and is assured by the wise Mrs. Hendrick that the baby needs no attention till 2:30. Following a feeding at this time there are three possible patterns which seem to follow: (1) awake and willing to remain fairly quiet, looking around or fussing intermittently; (2) continues nap on his back; (3) fussing or "a more vehement display." This last is the one that upsets young parents. What to do? In keeping with her philosophy ("It is not what the baby does . . . it is what you do about it") the author tells you exactly what to do.

I am convinced that this calm, firm, loving treatment is both possible and wonderfully comforting. The child learns from Day One that someone else is in charge, and can rest in that assurance. Isn't that what we all need throughout life? The knowledge that our lives are not haphazard but rather that we are loved with an Everlasting Love and that underneath are the Everlasting Arms? In other words, all is under control. The regular rhythm of holding, rocking, singing (Mrs. Hendrick includes all of that), bathing, feeding, changing, sleeping, playing, builds security. The child whose life is lived at random, governed by nothing more dependable than his own whims, is insecure and therefore unmanageable. His ego needs to be *bridled*. When the child is unmanageable the parents are in despair. When the parents are in despair the home is in chaos.

And I must add a little note here, while we're thinking about necessary restraints, to include a very useful invention of my mother's to keep a baby well covered in his crib. She made long cotton nightgowns with a drawstring in the bottom. She tied the string to a slat at the foot of the crib (I pinned it to the mattress for my baby—her crib didn't have slats). The baby was free to move all around but not up toward the head of the crib and out of the covers. The covers were tucked in at the sides, of course, and fastened at the top edges with blanket clips or large safety pins tied to the slats.

But why all this to introduce the subject of courtesy? Well, because courtesy begins with the realization that the world does not revolve around ourselves. We have to think of others. A baby thinks only of himself and his wants, but can soon learn that he is not in charge. His parents are. It is they who control what he gets and when. This is a good start for a child's learning not only to respect authority but also to think of others.

Not all children are given such a good start. One evening about eight o'clock I visited the home of a young couple. Both were seated on the floor with the baby. As we talked, they explained that the baby did not like to go to bed before nine, and it took both of them to get her there then. This was apparently all right with them, but I wondered if they wouldn't have enjoyed a quiet evening once in a while. And was it a good thing for the baby? I don't think it was. When the baby determines the schedule the whole family is heading for trouble.

Parents who love their children are willing to sacrifice for them. These young parents were sacrificing their freedom in the evenings for the sake of entertaining a baby who would have been much better off asleep. But the baby "did not like to go to bed before nine." She could have been trained, however, to go to bed at six. Loving parents sacrifice, but loving parents also train in order that the family may be knit together in love.

What does family love look like? St. Paul gives a picture of it:

> Being like-minded, having the same love, being one in spirit and purpose. Do nothing out of selfish ambition or vain conceit, but in humility consider others better than yourselves. Each of you should look not only to your own interests, but also to the interests of others.
>
> Your attitude should be the same as that of Christ Jesus: Who, being in very nature God, did not consider equality with God something to be grasped, but made himself nothing, taking the very nature of a servant (Phil. 2:2–7 NIV).

Someone has said that civilization is an exercise in self-restraint. My daughter and I lived with a jungle people considered highly uncivilized by outsiders, yet on the very first evening of our arrival they gave us all they had to give—a house, wood for a fire, water, and a supper of fish and manioc. In our two years there I learned a great deal from their example of self-restraint. With no idea of "etiquette" they were kind, generous, peaceful, easy to live with. I never heard them complain. Three wives of one man lived next door to me. They were the best of friends. I never heard a cross word between them.

There were no words in jungle languages for *please, thank you*, and *you're welcome*. This always left a sort of hole in the conversation to me, *please* having been one of the first words I learned as a baby, and the other expressions soon after. I was used to acknowledging others' kindness.

The word *manners* comes from the Latin *manus* meaning "hand." It is to *take in hand* and do things in a certain way. My mother and father took us in hand, individually and collectively, as they instilled into us the obligations of living under their roof.

"When *I* grow up I'm not going to make *my* children do thus and so," we sometimes said. The reply was simple: "Maybe so. But as long as you live in *our* house this is the way you'll do it!"

It was a daily exercise. Line upon line. Precept upon precept. We were reminded, corrected, urged, helped. Each rule was a good bridle for our egos. We needed those bridles.

Why must I sit up straight, keep elbows off the table and napkin in lap? Why does it matter that I eat quietly and chew with my mouth closed? Why shouldn't I talk with my mouth full? Why can't I reach for what I want? Why pass the butter to my brother first if I need some too?

The basic answer is that it makes things more pleasant for everybody. "Only a great fool or a great genius is likely to flout all social grace with impunity, and neither one, doing so, makes the most comfortable companion," says Amy Vanderbilt. Children do learn, and soonest taught soonest learned. Training six children is not six times as difficult as training one, for the younger ones learn even more quickly from each other than they do from their parents. I know several large families of young children who know how to behave at the table. A meal with families who don't is an ordeal.

Manners, said Emerson, are made up of petty sacrifices.

"Love has good manners and does not pursue selfish advantage" (1 Cor. 13:5 PHILLIPS).

A simple gesture like passing the butter plate to someone else before helping oneself is the outward expression, small and unobtrusive but deeply telling, of the sacrificial principle, "My life for yours." When there are only a few muffins left, the one who passes up the second helping lives out the words "in humility consider others better than yourselves." A child can easily learn the gesture. When he wants to know why it matters, he can be taught the Bible verse. It's someone else's comfort I should be concerned about, not my own.

At the supper table we were sometimes asked about our schoolwork or the happenings of the day, but were not expected to interrupt others or dominate the conversation. We learned to listen. When we had guests, which was often, my father was keenly interested in them and always tried to draw out as much as possible about their lives and work. The impression these stories made on us was deep and lasting.

While in our family there were plenty of times of uproarious laughter, times when we were allowed to play Hide and Seek in the house on a rainy day, times when we could not help shouting, running, jumping, and thundering up and down the stairs, we were taught to *think* first—was someone asleep, was Daddy studying, did Mother have a headache? Quietness was the general rule. Gentle voices, soft footsteps, the quiet closing of doors contribute to the peace of the home. Learning these simple things is learning to look to the interests of others rather than to one's own. If we thoughtlessly slammed a door (it was *so* hard to remember that big screen door in the summertime) we were asked to come back into the house and do it right.

The love that does not pursue selfish advantage respects the property and protects the privacy of others. Here was a lesson to be learned early because I never had a room of my own, which meant that there were boundaries sometimes difficult to keep—her side of the closet, my side, her drawers, mine. Each of us had his own towel and washcloth in the bathroom, always to be hung neatly on the racks. Why? Consideration of others. What kind of a bathroom do you want to come into? Recently I saw a lady in a public restroom wipe the sink with her paper towel. I commented on how extraordinary this was nowadays. "It's just a habit, I guess!" she laughed. Blessings on her parents!

Give up.
Give in.
Give way.
Give thanks.
Be ye kind.
Wait your turn.
Serve one another in love.

"The fruit of the Spirit is love, joy, peace, patience, kindness, goodness, faithfulness, gentleness and self-control" (Gal. 5:22–23 NIV). It is in the littlest things that these fruits are most often exhibited. This is courtesy—a glimpse of the Mystery of Charity.

CHAPTER 27

A
MOTHER'S
DEVOTION

Mother did not think of herself as deeply spiritual. She would have protested if anyone had said she was. But she was certainly hungry for God, deeply conscious of her own weakness and need of Him. Called to be a mother, entrusted with the holy task of cooperating with God in shaping the destinies of six people, she knew it was too heavy a burden to carry alone. She did not try. She went to Him whose name is Wonderful Counsellor, Mighty God, Everlasting Father. She asked His help.

She asked—daily. Not very early in the morning as my father did (she had no commuter train to catch), but after the children left for school she went to her appointment with the Lord. I don't know when I first became aware of this. It was probably not in Germantown but perhaps in the house on Oak Avenue. Mother always had her "little rocker" as she called it, in her bedroom, next to the little antique sewing table which stood under the window. On top of its crisp white linen cover was the neat stack of Bible, hymnbook, and the small red prayer notebook with a pen handy. Mother, as erect as Whistler's mother, sat in her rocking chair, reading, singing softly, praying, and occasionally jotting something in the margin of her Bible or in the notebook.

I have told how Daddy and Mother began their married life with prayer together, and how, later on, they gathered us daily, morning, evening, and at bedtime, for prayer. These were stones laid in the foundation of the home they shaped. Another was their individual prayer life. There is no doubt that the influences in the first eight or ten years of a child's life pretty well determine his future course. Whoever spends most of his waking hours with him is the principal moulder of his character. This was God's plan when He created Eve to be the mother of the race and Adam to husband (to protect, provide for, and cherish) her. Mother was not only there for *us*. She was regularly there, keeping her appointment with *God*—for us. Like her Lord Jesus, for *our* sakes she sanctified herself.

She read the Bible—read it, prayed over it ("Wonderful Counsellor, open Thy word to my heart. Open my heart to Thy word"), marked it, quoted it, asked the Lord to help her to understand, remember, and live by it. She believed every word of it to be inspired by God, profitable for doctrine, for reproof, for correction, for instruction in righteousness.

We would have said that Mother *always* read her Bible and prayed after breakfast. But of course it is not possible for anyone to keep perfectly to a schedule, especially with a large family. There were also lapses of another sort, as a poem of which she herself is apparently the author indicates:

> How cold the heart and stony—like one dead—
> On which the beams of God's own Word,
> In daily meditation fail to shed their warmth.
>
> If through neglect, we draw not near that fire,
> At first, unnoticed, creeps a shivering chill,
> But when neglected lies the Book for days,
> That chill takes hold, till the whole soul is ill.
>
> And yet when once again we seek God's Word,
> With empty heart and soul in deep despair,
> In faithfulness He meets us—praise the Lord!—
> And pours in oil and wine on all our care.

As her children grew, so Mother's sense of need for this faithful prayer time grew. Only the last of her small notebooks has survived, but it is a revelation of her desire for God

and her hopes for her children. The first page has the prayer
of King David when the temple was about to be built (Mother
always capitalized all pronouns referring to the Trinity, even
though the Authorized Version does not):

> Thine, O Lord, is the greatness and the power and the glory
> and the victory and the majesty; for all that is in the heaven
> and in the earth is Thine; Thine is the kingdom, O Lord, and
> Thou art exalted as head above all. Both riches and honor come
> of Thee, and Thou reignest over all, and in Thine hand is
> power and might and in Thine hand it is to make great and to
> give strength unto all. Now therefore, our God, we thank Thee
> and praise Thy glorious Name (1 Chron. 29:11–13 av).

Underneath she put a reference to the last stanza of an Amy
Carmichael poem from *Toward Jerusalem:*

> Therefore we come, Thy righteousness our cover,
>   Thy precious Blood our one, our only plea.
> Therefore we come, O Savior, Master, Lover.
>   To whom, Lord, could we come save unto Thee?

There are prayer lists for each day of the week, with the
names of us six at the top of each. Mother often prayed the
words of 1 Chronicles 29:19 for her sons: "Give unto ———,
my son, a perfect heart to keep Thy commandments, Thy
testimonies, and Thy statutes." A tiny footnote says, "This
goes for Betty and Ginny also, of course." She had a long list
of Christian organizations of all kinds, referring to them by
their initials—PBI, HDA, LAM, SST, SIM, NYBS, ABWE,
NCEM, etc.—whose needs she spread before God. She prayed
by name for many missionaries. She remembered the Christian schools and colleges her children attended. Billy and
Ruth Graham, friends of my parents for years, are on her
Tuesday list, a granddaughter's Bible class on Thursday. Fri-
days she gave especially to confession, citing pride, criticism,
doubt, lack of love and thanksgiving, coldness, disobedience.
With that last one, she notes Deuteronomy 11:26–27: "I set
before you this day a blessing . . . if you obey the commandments of the Lord your God, which I command you this

day." She prayed for grace on the basis of Romans 5:20, "Where sin abounded, grace did much more abound."

Mother made great use of hymns. She knew scores, perhaps hundreds, of hymns by heart, read them, prayed through them, and sang them by herself, in spite of her voice's weakening and quavering in later years. The notebook quotes a good many. Here is one which took on special meaning after her "chicks" had flown, I. S. Stevenson's hymn of 1869:

> Holy Father, in Thy mercy,
> Hear our anxious prayer;
> Keep our loved ones, now far distant,
> 'Neath Thy care.

> Jesus, Savior, let Thy presence
> Be their light and guide;
> Keep, O keep them, in their weakness
> At Thy side.

> When in sorrow, when in danger,
> When in loneliness,
> In Thy love look down and comfort
> Their distress.

> May the Joy of Thy salvation
> Be their strength and stay;
> May they love and may they praise Thee
> Day by day.

> Holy Spirit, let Thy teaching
> Sanctify their life;
> Send Thy grace that they may conquer
> In the strife.

> Father, Son, and Holy Spirit,
> God the One in Three,
> Bless them, guide them, save them, keep them
> Near to Thee.

Mothers today who feel that their work has been devalued by the world will find encouragement in these lines (for which Mother gave no source):

In this little time does it matter,
As we work, and we watch, and we wait,
If we're filling the place He assigns us,
Be it labor small or great?

Like most of us, Mother was often nettled by the question
of whether feelings and experiences were a valid gauge to her
growth in grace. She and I talked about this many times, both
of us sure that if our "spirituality" or our acceptance with
God depended on thrills and chills, we were of all women
most miserable. We could not conjure up the feelings. She
noted three passages which helped her. The first is from J. I.
Packer's *Knowing God:*

It is not as we strain after feelings and experiences . . . but
as we seek God Himself, looking to Him as our Father, prizing
His fellowship, and finding in ourselves an increasing concern
to know and *please* Him, that the reality of the Spirit's ministry
becomes visible in our lives. This is the needed truth which can
lift us out of the quagmire of non-spiritual views of the Spirit
in which so many today are floundering.

The second is from Evan Hopkins's little book *Broken Bread*:

Are we ever tempted to think that because of fluctuating
feelings and harassing doubts, we are no longer acceptable to
God? Let us remember that it is never because of anything in
us that we are accepted at all. The measure of our acceptance is
what Christ is to God; and that remains ever the same.

And another from George MacDonald:
"The highest condition of the human will is when, not seeing God, not seeming to grasp Him at all, we yet hold Him
fast."
George MacDonald had not been a part of my father's library, but we came to know him later when a friend began
sending me the original editions of his wonderful novels.
Mother loved them and found in them, as I have, much which
corrected and shaped her spiritual understanding. She quoted
from *What's Mine's Mine*:
" 'Nothing good will come of it,' she said . . .

" 'Everything good will come of it, Mother, that God would have come of it.' "

From *Warlock of Glenwarlock*:

> She suffered from rheumatism, which she described as a "sorrow in her bones." But she never lost her patience and so got the good of a trouble which would seem specially sent as the concluding discipline of old people for this world, that they may start well in the next.
>
> There is no escaping the mill that grinds slowly and grinds small, and those who refuse to be living stones in the living temple must be ground into mortar for it.

A tattered mimeographed copy of an anonymous poem is pasted on a page of the notebook. It contains a maxim which Mother found greatly comforting and fortifying in all kinds of circumstances, especially the kind that would tend toward the paralysis which self-pity brings:

> From an old English parsonage down by the sea
> There came in the twilight a message to me;
> Its quaint Saxon legend, deeply engraven,
> Hath, it seems to me, teaching from Heaven.
> And on through the hours the quiet words ring
> Like a low inspiration: "DOE THE NEXTE THYNGE."
>
> Many a questioning, many a fear,
> Many a doubt, hath its quieting here.
> Moment by moment, let down from Heaven,
> Time, opportunity, guidance, are given.
> *Fear not tomorrows*, child of the King,
> *Trust them with Jesus, doe the nexte thynge.*
>
> Do it immediately, do it with prayer;
> Do it reliantly, casting all care;
> Do it with reverence, tracing His hand
> Who placed it before thee with earnest command.
> Stayed on Omnipotence, safe 'neath His wing,
> Leave all resultings, *doe the nexte thynge.*
>
> Looking to Jesus, ever serener,
> Working or suffering, be thy demeanor;

In His dear presence, the rest of His calm,
The light of His countenance be thy psalm,
Strong in His faithfulness, praise and sing.
Then, as He beckons thee, *doe the nexte thynge*

Mother noted down sketchy outlines of what she was learning from the Scriptures—how God directs our way (to the listening ear, Isa. 30:21; the empty hand, Isa. 41:13; the willing feet, Luke 1:79); what the name of the God of Jacob does for us—sixteen things from Psalm 20; a study of the "greater than's"; the importance of obedience from the life of Esther; John Stott's five marks of God's people: growth, fellowship, worship, witness, holiness.

She quotes Robert Browning's poem "The best is yet to be," and Einstein's theory of relativity: "the amalgamation of space, time, and matter into one fundamental unity," to which she appends Hebrews 1:3, "upholding all things by the word of His power," and Colossians 1:17, "And He is before all things and by Him all things consist."

One tiny notation sends a deep pang to my heart as I write this book. With a red pen Mother wrote my initials and a date (alas—I remember the pain I was causing her then, but I can thank God for His grace and mercy today) in the margin next to Christina Rossetti's words,

My faith burns low, my hope
burns low;
Only my heart's desire cries
out in me,
By the deep thunder of its
want and woe,
Cries out to Thee.

At the bottom she wrote, "No might—we know not what to do—our eyes are upon Thee. II Chron. 20:12."

CHAPTER 28

LETTING
US
GROW

We never were *teen-agers*. I can't help being very thankful that the term had not been thought of in my day. I think it spared us some silliness and some real pain. It has become an accepted label for a stage in life usually dreaded by parents and relished by children as a time when anything goes. But this is an invention of modern times and affluent societies. Jesus, at the age of twelve, deliberately set about His Father's business. Jewish boys at thirteen mark a clear transition from child to adult in the Bar Mitzvah. King Josiah was eight years old when he began to reign, and at sixteen the Bible says that he began to seek the God of his father David. At twenty he took strong and sweeping action against the idolatry rampant in Judah at the time. Indian boys of the jungle tribes I knew in Ecuador shouldered the burden of bringing in wild meat for the tribe when they were nine or ten. In another two years or so they were looked upon as men, with all the responsibilities manhood meant—hunting, fishing, and warring to protect the community and, very soon, their own families. There was no time or inclination for doing nothing.

Our world was a different one, of course, but not as different from the Indians' world then as it is now. How did we survive those years between ten and twenty which seem to hold such shock waves for youth and the parents of youth

today? Well, for one thing, we always had to "get at things."
That was my mother's expression. We teased her about it
often, and she took our teasing with good grace, setting an
example for all of us, for we were a teasing family. Nowadays
such teasing would be called putting people down, very bad
for the psyche or something. It was good for us—you only
tease people you love. And we learned to laugh at ourselves.

Getting at things meant doing the next thing, whatever
needed to be done, and doing it now. We got a lot of work
done fast so that we could go on to things we could enjoy
even more because we'd done the work first. That was good
for us too.

We were not taught to expect a stage of chaos and rebellion.
Some prophecies are self-fulfilling. If they're never heard,
they never happen. It's amazing how much simpler life was
without television! We did not know we were supposed to
kick over all the traces, go completely wild, declare our inde-
pendence, defy our elders, do our own thing. We did not
know we had reached an uncontrollable stage, everything at
the boiling point, everything up for grabs.

There are physical and psychological changes which today
we call "major." That word in itself is like an alarm. We jump
and prepare for the worst. Nothing was "major" in my parents' vocabulary. They didn't know enough to be worried
about psychology. They did their best to prepare us for the
physical changes, and their best was good enough, I think. It
did not include vivid pictures, detailed discussions, or plant-
ing in our minds the idea that sexuality is a *problem*. It was
God's wonderful design, something to be looked forward to.
They never had to tell us sex was meant only for marriage. If
we heard of it in any other context we knew it was wrong.

My mother answered my questions quite simply as they
arose. When I was seven she explained that we would be
having a baby in the house in a few months, and that that
baby was growing inside her. I had no idea that my father
had anything to do with this astonishing business until the
next baby was on the way, when another question brought
forth her answer. A year or so later, she took me on a long car
trip where we had quiet time to explain menstruation and a

few details about married love. It was my father, I think, who explained things to the boys. We had a book called *Growing Up*, meant to teach children the basic facts of life. I think I would have learned more from Margaret Clarkson's book *Susie's Babies*, which wasn't available back then.

Terrible things have happened in the decades of the mass media. Who can deny that the greater the dissemination of the *knowledge* of evil the greater the harvest? Parents are drawn into a more desperate warfare than ever before against its effects on the minds of their children. When from every side the message is IF IT FEELS GOOD DO IT! it takes constant reiteration of the great practical and joy-giving principles of self-denial and purity and obedience to counteract it.

❦

Parents have asked me what sort of punishments I might recommend for children who are beyond the spanking age. They don't know what to do with teen-agers. What did my parents do? I couldn't think of a thing. I asked my sister and brothers. Nobody can remember any punishments such as "grounding," fines, withholding the car keys (we seldom got them anyway—we never had more than one car for the whole tribe), or anything else. Isn't this just "the proof of the pudding"? Training given *early* enough, *consistently* enough has long-term effects. It wasn't that we were "good kids." It's just that we got the message. No other explanation seems possible.

Our parents' ultimate goal in their discipline, the goal of anyone who teaches anything, is that the pupil may be led by degrees to self-discipline and become a law to himself. I for one am thankful for the habits they taught me, for habits are powerful things—work, prayer, obedience, churchgoing, "eating your spinach before you eat dessert"—these things have helped me through all my life.

For many years my father wrote editorials (which we knew as "ed notes") for *The Sunday School Times*. They were concise, practical, and often sprang from his immediate experience. In one of them he said,

The trouble with so many parents is that they do not begin early enough to insist on obedience, telling the truth, and respect for parents; and unfortunately many do not behave in the home in ways that inspire respect. Love, kindness, cheerfulness, and good times should abound in every Christian home, but these are stifled where there is disobedience, disrespect, and where the children's will dominates. Parents are God's representatives in the home and, like Him, they should keep the right balance between Law and grace.

It is no easy task to manage the wills of children without yielding to whims or provoking resistance. A great educator wrote,

> It must be recognized from the beginning that the work is slow; if it is forced on too fast either a breaking point comes and the child, too much teased into perfection, turns in reaction and becomes self-willed and rebellious; or if, unhappily, the forcing process succeeds, a little paragon is produced . . . On the other hand, if those who have to bring up children, fear too much to cross their inclinations, and so seek always the line of least resistance, teaching lessons in play, and smoothing over every rough place of the road, the result is a weak, slack will, a mind without power of concentration, and in later life very little resourcefulness in emergency or power of bearing up under difficulties or privations. (Janet Erskine Stuart, *The Education of Catholic Girls*, pp. 33f.)

Of the making of books on child training there is no end. Of discussions about which method works best there is no end. I have not meant to add to those books or settle the arguments, but simply to present what one pair of Christian parents actually did. The question will be asked, Did their method *work*? How shall I answer? I can say that we grew up in a peaceful home. I can't think of any quality more to be desired than that, for it was the peace of the Lord. We did a lot of laughing. We had fun. We loved our parents, and they loved us. We told the truth. I think all of us are almost physically incapable of looking someone in the eye and lying. I have included the story of my one foiled attempt to steal something. Phil wrote from the army to thank Mother and Dad for training him to obey, for he was not tempted to break the rules as others were. The principles our parents taught are a part of the warp and woof of our lives.

If the questioner persists and asks, Did no one ever *rebel*? the answer is we are sinners. The sinful nature with which we are born is a rebellious nature, and I'm sure I was not the only one who had at times a very rebellious spirit, like that of the small boy who when told to sit on a chair as a punishment, obediently sat, but declared he was "standing up on the inside." Our failures, which have been many, are not due to our parents' failure to show us the right way.

My grandfather, Philip E. Howard, wrote a little gem of a book called *The Many-Sided David*. In his chapter on the Absalom story, "The King with the Father Heart," he says,

> A boy who counts heredity an excuse for sin is no sounder in his reckoning than the father who thinks himself blameless for the misdeeds of the son. A father can never be what he ought to be to his son until he frankly accepts personal responsibility before God and man for his share in the son's personality.
>
> On the other hand, a son can never be the man he might be until he utterly refuses to admit the fallacy that his father's sins impair or modify his own relation to Christ, in whom he will find not a mere ethic and example, but an empowering personality that never staggers at heredity in giving a son newness of life. Christ does not offer himself to a young man with reservations conditioned upon the father's belief or habits . . .
>
> A modern Christian student of human nature, Mr. Patterson DuBois, reviews the unscientific so-called "laws" of heredity, and concludes with this clear word based upon his studies of the subject: "Let no individual either rest content in, or stand in dread of the unknowable factor of his own heredity."
>
> . . . Do we who are sons not know that it is fatal to character to rest for spiritual strength in our father's spiritual life, or to set limits to Christ's work for us by the measure of ancestral weakness?

For the physical life they gave us and the spiritual life they showed us, for all the ways in which we have been made rich because our father and mother quite literally laid down their lives for us, I thank God. I have no reason to believe they pray less for us now than they did when they lived on earth. Surely they must continue their cooperative work with God, asking that He will keep on shaping us to the image of His Son.

CHAPTER 29

LETTING
US
GO

*I*t was not easy for our parents to let us go. They knew from the start that they were trustees, not owners, of the children God had given them. We were not their property. We had been lent to them for a time, a sacred trust of which they were the divinely assigned trustees. A time came when that trust had been discharged. Relinquishing the spiritual reins must have been the hardest thing for parents like mine whose primary concern had always been to set our hearts on things above. What if our vision began to sink to things of earth? They could not possibly monitor our thinking, but the temptation would be strong to feel that they ought to be doing *something* more than praying.

Before we reached the age of twelve they were fairly assured that each of us had made a commitment to Christ. They had done their part in this, but knew that no father or mother can convert a child. Conversion is the work of God. It is a new birth, one which depends "not on natural descent nor on any physical impulse or plan of man, but on God" (John 1:13 PHILLIPS). I don't believe our parents could have made this any clearer to us than they did.

But the time comes when that childhood decision must be examined. Mother and Daddy backed off then, knowing their role was now prayer more than anything else, prayer that God would fulfil in their children the covenant He made with the house of Israel, "I will put my laws *in their minds* and write them *on their hearts.* I will be their God, and they will be my people" (Heb. 8:10 NIV, italics mine).

George MacDonald wrote,

> Every generation must do its own seeking and its own find-ing. The fault of the fathers often is that they expect their find-ing to stand in place of their children's seeking. They expect the children to receive that which has satisfied the need of their fathers upon their testimony; whereas rightly, their testimony is not ground for their children's belief, only for their children's search. That search is faith in the bud. (*The Miracles of Our Lord,* pp. 78f.)

MacDonald's remarks are in the context of the story in John 4 of the official from Capernaum who comes to Jesus in Cana, begging Him to come and heal his son who is at the point of death. Jesus gives him His word that the son will live. The official believes the word, goes home, finds that the fever had left his son at the very time when Jesus spoke. To the father it was without question a miracle. The servants and the son, on the other hand, may perhaps have dismissed it as a coinci-dence, for they had not themselves seen the Lord and heard Him speak. They had no ground but the father's testimony.

From the ground of our parents' testimony we Howards have gone in many different directions in our individual searchings, yet when we met together in 1990, the youngest of us being then fifty years old, we spent hours talking, with great affection and gratitude, of home and parents and all they had given us. Some of us find ourselves reverting more and more to that wonderful legacy. Tom recently had dinner with two friends who came from homes similar to ours. All three men agreed that though they had diverged in varying measure from the ways in which they had been trained, they found themselves becoming more like their fathers every day. This was something of a surprise and a revelation for them as they talked. Perhaps it was a quite literal fulfilment of the ancient proverb about training a child in the way he should go, "and when he is *old* he will not depart from it."

It was not until after my parents' deaths that I learned that my decision, after graduation from college, to identify myself with a group commonly (though not "officially") called Plymouth Brethren, was a severe shock and sorrow to both of them. It was not that they thought I had left the faith. They respected the Brethren but had certain misgivings. They could not have helped feeling (I would feel this in their place) that I regarded their training and example as not quite up to par. I'm afraid that is exactly what I did think. They questioned me kindly, of course, but to their credit they never let me know how they felt, nor did they admonish me, as they certainly would have done if they had believed I was taking a course which would be spiritually disastrous.

Their first great "letting go" took place in 1941. Both Phil and Dave had attended the Stony Brook School earlier (for a year each, I think), but that was on Long Island, New York, not very far from home. In 1941 Phil went to Prairie Bible Institute in Alberta, Canada, and I went to Hampden DuBose Academy in Orlando, Florida. Travel was by train (air travel was for the rich only) in those days. Alberta and Florida might as well have been the North Pole and the South Pacific.

We knew we had to stay for nine months. There would be no trips home for Christmas or Easter vacations, and as for phone calls, we never dreamed of calling long distance. That too was for the rich except in the direst of emergencies.

Phil was seventeen, I was fourteen. Daddy and Mother had confidence in the spiritual standards of both institutions. L. E. Maxwell, founder and principal of Prairie, was a sound Bible teacher and a personal friend. The DuBoses had invited our Uncle Charley to speak at HDA, so we knew they "couldn't be all bad." He had brought us a copy of their yearbook, filled with appealing photos of beautiful Florida—palm trees, white sand beaches, serene lakes, girls in formal dresses, boys in white suits, small classes seated on the grass with young and pretty teachers. I pored over those photos for hours, seeing myself in a long gown amidst the azaleas. I longed to go. We talked it over for some weeks. A boarding school? Why? Well, it was a Christian one. There were no Christian day schools that we knew of. I had no Christian friends in my class in public school. I felt very much left out. My parents hoped that the training at HDA would confirm and strengthen the training they had tried to give me (it did). These seemed good reasons, but financially it was out of the question. However, Uncle Charley's death not long after put my father in the position of editor of *The Sunday School Times*, raised his salary, and enabled him to pay the three hundred dollars which covered room, board, and tuition.

Mother's autobiography says,

ເ໑ With Betty's and Phil's departure for two schools of similar religious basis, but extreme contrasts in outward appearance and social ideas, began a time described by the youngest member of the family in later years of "suitcases bumping up and down the stairs"! BUMP went the suitcases as the wanderers returned for the summer holidays. THUMP and SCRATCH as they were pulled down the stairs for departure! Those were days when we wiped tears surreptitiously as the West Coast Champion pulled away heading south, or the Trail Blazer headed west, or the Greyhound bus roared off with one or other of our beloved bairns. ໑໐

Letting go did not mean crossing us off. Mother wrote to Phil and me faithfully, a letter every Sunday and a post card every Wednesday. Mail at the Academy was put into alphabetically marked pigeon holes. I seized the "H's" and whipped through them eagerly. The sight of Mother's smooth round handwriting made me very happy. I am sorry now that I never thought of saving those cards and letters, not even one. They were always full of family doings and expressions of love, and usually included some encouraging word from Scripture or a hymn or poem that might meet me where I was. One of those poems survived because I memorized it and copied it into my Bible (I do not know the source, but guess it may be Martha Snell Nicholson):

As Any Mother to the Savior

As Thou didst walk the lanes of Galilee,
So, loving Savior, walk with her for me,

For since the years have passed and she is grown,
I cannot follow; she must walk alone.

Be Thou my feet that I have had to stay,
For Thou canst comrade her on every way;
Be Thou my voice when sinful things allure,
Pleading with her to choose those which endure.
Be Thou my hands that would keep hers in mine,
And all things else that mothers must resign.

When she was little, I could walk and guide,
But now I pray that Thou be at her side.
And as Thy blessed mother folded Thee,
So, loving Savior, fold my girl for me.

My father also wrote to me now and then. He quoted to me one of his favorite Bible verses, Isaiah 41:10, "Fear thou not; for I am with thee: be not dismayed; for I am thy God: I will strengthen thee; yea, I will help thee; yea, I will uphold thee with the right hand of my righteousness" (AV).

When Peter Marshall was about to leave for his first job away from home his mother walked with him to the little iron gate.

"Dinna forget your verse, my laddie," she said. " 'Seek ye first the kingdom of God and His righteousness, and all these things shall be added unto you.' Long ago I pit ye in the Lord's hands, and I'll no be takin' ye awa noo. He will tak' care o' you. Dinna worry."

And thus my dear parents *pit* us each one into those same hands, nor did they ever *tak' us awa*.

CHAPTER 30

THE MATTER OF MARRIAGE

When my brother Jim asked Dad for suggestions for a prayer list my father told him he should be praying about the two most important decisions still facing him which were, in order of importance, a wife, and his life's work. The supremely important decision—that of binding himself to Christ as Lord and Master—had long since been settled. Our parents had made the marriages of their children a matter of prayer for years, and daily had lived out before us the example of a truly Christian marriage. Not that we thought of it as such—we hardly knew there was another kind. When I began to dream of having a husband he was always a Christian husband. That was axiomatic. We knew what the Bible says about the "unequal yoke."

Because we had known from earliest childhood the Holy Scriptures and been taught and encouraged in every possible way to surrender our lives to Christ, the adolescent years, so much dreaded by many parents today, were not nearly so dangerous for us as they would have been without the spiritual care that had been so earnestly given. We had "anchors." We had, as the soldier said to whom my father had offered a pocket Testament, something to "tie us down."

Mother had told us about her boyfriends, beginning with the little Quaker boy who carried a schoolbag.

ৎৡ NOBODY carried a SCHOOLBAG! He would try to meet me after school to walk with me. To avoid him I would sneak around a different way, but sometimes he would spot me and then I'd hear him running behind me with his schoolbag thumping up and down on his back. I would then take off like a gazelle and the race was hardly a fair one as I was light on my feet and he was anything but. One time I did accept an invitation from him to attend a Saturday afternoon performance of the Philadelphia Orchestra. His Aunt Hannah Morris chaperoned us and she was a truly delightful woman who lived in the famous Morris Mansion on Germantown Avenue.

Then there was Johnny, son of the Episcopal rector. I remember him sitting talking to me in the parlor at Green Street and I would get so-o sleepy I would be cross-eyed. He didn't notice (I hope) as he loved to have an audience . . . Bob was very faithful. When in the ROTC during World War I he asked me to "wait for him." I just laughed him off, which really was unkind as I am sure he was quite serious. He took me to some of the nicest things, too—the Fortnightly Club and interesting lectures.

Wis Wood was also around a lot and once suggested the possibility of our hitting it off for life! As we usually spent any time we were together in hot arguments, I assured him I had no intention of spending my life debating with him. ৡৎ

There were other boyfriends we heard about, and I think I counted three proposals. So Mother spoke with authority when she gave me two specific instructions regarding boys:

1. Never chase them.
2. Keep them at arm's length.

There was a whole worldview in those simple maxims, a vision of God's order in the making of men and women. Harmony, not unison. Glorious inequalities, not equality. Complementarity, not interchangeability. One the operator, the other the cooperator. Eve was made for Adam, not Adam for Eve. Christ is the Bridegroom, represented in marriage by the husband as the one who is responsible, to woo and to win, to call his bride to himself and give her his name, to cherish and protect and provide for her by sacrificing himself. All that would have been over my head when I was ten or twelve, but I could perfectly well understand "Never chase them." I took the advice.

The second rule has made sense to many besides my mother. When Henry Brandt the psychologist's children were teens, they objected to the requirement that cars were to be used for transportation only and not for entertaining. He urged them to keep some "daylight" between bodies. His son's impassioned question was, "Don't you trust me?"

His answer: "Absolutely not. When you are using one third of the seat for both of you, touching that warm body with her blood running hot and your blood boiling, I should say I *don't* trust you. Put me in the same position with the girl's mother, I wouldn't trust *me*. In fact," he says now at the age of seventy-four, "put me in the same position with the girl's grandmother and I wouldn't trust me. Each caress, each kiss, has a cumulative effect. Kiss power is stronger than will power."

Mother would have said Amen to that. Her rule made sense to me because monogamy made sense to me. One woman for one man, and no trespassing until that one was declared and committed. Why risk the dangers of no-man's-land? Hold your distance. Maintain the mystery. Keep them guessing. Don't give them anything to work on.

I took that advice too. My being extremely shy and very tall precluded her having many worries along these lines. I was a head taller than nearly all of the boys until I reached high school, so none of them were chasing me and I would rather have died than chase them. I don't remember the subject of dating arising at all until Halloween when I was in the eighth grade. A plump red-haired boy named Ned who was almost as tall as I was asked me to go to a party. I was overcome. Oh wonderful. Oh marvelous. Betty Howard? Asked for a date? But oh *dear*. Would I know what to talk about? What if I bored him? What would I wear?

Mother was pleased and calm and matter-of-fact in trying to help me see that it would all work perfectly well if I simply forgot myself and asked questions about things he was interested in. Ned was to come to our house, of course, and I must bring him into the living room to meet Mother and Daddy. We were to be home by ten o'clock. Nothing disastrous must have happened that evening, for I remember absolutely nothing except that I wore a new pair of brown suede shoes, my first "heels," and silk stockings.

That was it for a while. Nobody asked me for a date in ninth grade, and in tenth grade I was at boarding school, where we girls were not likely to be flattered when asked, because there were only certain specified occasions when dating was allowed, and on those we knew that the boys, poor things, were more or less required to ask us—and we were not permitted to refuse.

Long before my sister Ginny went to HDA it was apparent that hers would be a different story from mine. She started out in kindergarten or first grade letting little Richie Bartello carry her lunchbox when he walked her home from school, and from then on had enough boys hovering around to keep my parents on their toes, or rather on their knees.

I'm not sure what my brothers did about girls. My impression is that they did very little. Phil's first love was trains. He spent a lot of time riding his bike along Third Street next to the railroad track, wearing his engineer's cap, keeping up with the trains as they moved slowly through town. He knew the schedules to the minute, knew some of the engine crews by name, and was even invited on occasion to ride with them. He could identify all the engine types and did a perfect imitation of steam engine noises. Obviously he had no time for girls—except Susie. But that was earlier. When Phil and Susie McCutcheon were both ten they rode the trolley and subway into Philadelphia to spend the day. My father received a distress call at his office from Susie's father: "Your son has my daughter down there in the city and they've run out of money." The two fathers found the careless pair sitting on a newsstand, swinging their legs, feeding peanuts to the pigeons. The cost of the peanuts had wiped out their return carfare. So much for chivalry.

One girl, hopeful for some sign from Tom which was not forthcoming, sidled up to him at last with a timid, "Somebody told me you like me." "Well," said Tom (he was in the fourth or fifth grade), "somebody told you *wrong*." So much for women who take the initiative.

One thing my father made crystal clear to his four sons: *never* tell a woman you love her until you are ready to follow that confession with an immediate proposal. Do a lot of praying and seeking the Lord's will in this all-important matter *before* you get involved. Then, in His time, say to her, "I love you. Will you marry me?" There is no question that this rule saved my brothers (and who knows how many girls?) many a heartache.

Theophan writes,

> Whoever has gone without danger through the years of youth has, as it were, sailed across a stormy river and, looking back, he blesses God. But someone else, with tears in his eyes, turns back in regret and curses himself. You will never recover what you have lost in your youth. Will one who has fallen ever again attain what is possessed by one who has not fallen? (*Raising Them Right*, p. 62)

Mother and Daddy went on praying—the right woman for each son, the right man for each daughter, at the *right time*. And of course they continually laid before the Lord our life's work, asking that each of us should seek His will above all.

The Second World War was still in progress when Phil graduated from PBI in 1944. Travel was almost impossible because trains were filled with troops, but Mother somehow managed to reserve a seat, and somehow she was able to buy a ticket to Alberta—no doubt a gift from the hand of God via one of His servants. Graduation at Prairie was held during Spring Conference when speakers were brought in and there was a strong appeal to all the students to consider seriously the foreign mission field. Mother wrote,

    I do not even remember who the other speakers (besides William Chisholm of Korea) were, nor what they said, but I returned home with a verse recurring to my mind over and over: "Pray ye the Lord of the harvest that He will send forth laborers into His harvest field"! Fine! O.K. I'd pray that! Little did I know what it would cost me! One day as I was praying that prayer a disturbing thought entered my mind: "Whose children are you going to pray Him to send?"

I shied away from the implications I could see were coming. It was some time before I could bring myself to pray in a very feeble way that He would send MY children into His field!

That fall Phil entered what was then called National Bible Institute in New York City. He wanted to take the missionary medical course in preparation for going, as he hoped, to the mission field, thoughts of China and Siberia being part of his thinking at that time.

A lovely little girl from Charlotte, North Carolina, was a student at the Bible school and Phil, who up to that time had had no eyes for girls, began to find her company quite pleasing. I had promised Ginny and Tommy, then ten and eight-and-a-half, that we would spend a weekend in New York while Phil was at NBI. Phil had arranged several trips to please his young sister and brother, and I was amazed (and pleased) to find that Margaret Funderburk was always included in these plans. Before returning home I asked Phil if he would like me to invite her to visit us on her way back to Charlotte. He looked surprised and pleased at the idea, and little urging was needed to get her consent. ᦕ

One evening while Margaret was in Moorestown, Mother and Phil had a talk.

ᦕ I asked him quite frankly how he felt about Margaret. There was a long silence and then he said, "What do you mean?" I tried to be very casual as I replied, "Well, suppose you never saw her again after she leaves here. Would it matter to you?" Another long silence and a brief, "I don't know. I never thought of it!!" The next day he took her by train to Keswick for the day and on their return as they walked from the station to our house I spied them coming along arm in arm!!! I have always been thankful for that day spent and the boatride on the lake when Phil put a very important question to our dear daughter-in-love, Margaret!   ☙

Margaret, slender, small, and very pretty, with blue eyes and beautiful, dark, naturally wavy hair, shared my bedroom. I watched her as she sat up in bed one night and wrote a letter ("a love letter!" I told myself) to Phil. It sobered me to think that she would be my big brother's wife. My sister-in-law. Nothing more important had ever happened at our house. Here was solemn evidence of the Lord's guidance, a business which I was wrestling with and worrying a good bit about. Would He lead *me* clearly? Would I know? Phil knew. When he returned from seeing her off at the train station I asked him if he was sure he loved her.

"I love that little gal like I never thought I could love ANY BODY!" he said. I could not doubt the word of a man with such a light in his eyes.

Would I be next? Mother and Daddy never asked me that question. They only asked God.

During my senior year of college Dave brought his friend Jim Elliot home for Christmas vacation with our family. Long talks after the others had gone to bed revealed that Jim and I had many things in common, but we had no such thing as a "relationship" for months to come. Mother wrote about what happened in June:

☙ In order to attend Betty's graduation, some extra wherewithal had to be scraped up from somewhere and so the big Rose Medallion punch bowl of my mother's was sold to defray expenses. That was not a happy graduation for me—in spite of Betty's fine record at college—for she told me when we got out there that she and Jim had found out they loved each other but that they would not ever see each other after graduation, as he felt he must serve God as a single man! . . . Dave's profound astonishment one night when he saw Betty and Jim going off together for the last time (as they thought) is impossible to describe. I remember it so well.   ☙

They liked Jim very much. My father said only one thing I remember about our situation: God is not the author of confusion. He and Mother prayed definitely and persistently for God's will for the two of us. The working out of that will is told elsewhere in detail (see *Passion and Purity*).

Next in the birth-order is Dave. Mother recounts:

   ∿ I have already described how I put my finger into the PGH pie! This next time was somewhat different, but equally astounding! The day before Dave was to leave home in the fall of 1949 to go into the Foreign Missions Fellowship of the Inter-Varsity Christian Fellowship, he and I were talking about his interest in the possibility of going into work in Afghanistan. I asked him if the men in that work felt it best for a missionary to be married or unmarried. Dave replied that they felt it best for a man to be married, but he then said, "I don't see how I will get to meet any girls in the work of FMF as I will be traveling all over the country and not staying long in any one place."

The next morning at family prayers Dad was praying especially for Dave as he faced the responsibilities of his new work with FMF and as he prayed the name of Phyllis Gibson flashed across my mind. After prayers Dad took off for his morning train and I turned to Dave and said quite casually and with no special *arrière penseé,* "Dave, whatever became of that girl you used to date at Wheaton named Phyllis Gibson?" (I might say that I remembered her mostly as a friend of Betty's whom she called "Gibby" and whom I may have met only once or twice.) I have often wished I had had a camera and could have preserved for posterity the amazed expression on Dave's face when I said that! He looked almost stunned! "Mother," he said, "I have not been able to get her out of my mind all summer and I have wondered if this was of the Lord, so I prayed, putting out a fleece that if it was His thought for me, that YOU would speak to me about her! This was the most impossible fleece I could think of!"

I guess my own expression may have been worth

photographing, too! I was dumfounded and thought, "Oh, what have I done?"

At lunch that day I piled the food onto Dave's plate as I usually did, but noticed that he only toyed with it. I finally said, "What's the matter, Dave? Don't you feel well?" "Yes, I'm O.K., but there are too many butterflies in my stomach!"

Hearing this amazing statement, Jimmy, then nine years old, turned to him excitedly and asked, "Dave, have you been eating butterflies?"

Well, when Dave arrived in Colorado where he was to begin his work with FMF the staff man there found out Dave wanted very much to visit a young lady in Montana and so made it possible for him to go. Not long after came a long-distance phone call announcing their engagement!

Parents' fingers can get into their children's pies in many ways. Probably the very best way was the way Dad's finger entered the pie of the romance between Tom and Lovelace!! It must have been about 1961 that he said to me one day, "I hope you will join me in praying that God will give Lovelace Oden to Tom for his wife!" LOVELACE ODEN!! I hardly knew her and besides she was a missionary in Japan under the CIM and Tom was our bachelor son teaching English to English boys in Kingsmead in England! They were on opposite sides of the world and I could see no possible way for such a thing to take place. (O me of little faith!) I replied that I had been praying that God would bring the woman of His choice into Tom's life, but I wasn't sure I could pinpoint it to the extent of asking that that woman be Lovelace. "Well, I can," replied Dad, "I feel quite sure about it!" He had met Lovelace when she was a candidate for the CIM and he was on the Council, and had been very impressed by her. I knew of her as having attended HDA and Wheaton, and that she and Tom had seen each other at these two schools, but I really didn't know her at all. From time to time over the next two years Dad would say to me, "I hope you are praying about Tom and Lovelace!" I always felt a bit guilty, as my faith did not come up to his in this matter. He did not live to see the answer to that prayer, but I'm sure he knows about it and rejoices!

And so it has been in the lives of our other three as far as their marriages are concerned. Prayer begun when they were still in their early teens, by their parents, was answered in individual ways since there is no fixed pattern for God's dealings with us.

Having successfully squashed the hopes of several young men who aspired to her heart, Ginny was swept into the arms of the glamorous president of the senior class of 1952 when she was a little freshman at Wheaton. It rather took our breath away at the time, but twenty years in the Philippines have been blessed of God in their work of translation and evangelism.

Dad and Jim and I went to New York to see Tom off on the ship that was to take him to England for two years of teaching. Jim had confided to him some hopes and fears about a certain young woman at Wheaton and Tom's parting word to him, a word of encouragement to go ahead with his hopes, seemed to give him the green light and God has surely blessed his union with his dear Joyce in many ways—four lovely children, two hundred acres of farmland in Minnesota, a comfortable home, and best of all, a little chapel where they have served God for some years with the joy of bringing help to many. The inbuilt appreciation for beauty and art still have their fulfilment in the work put out in the little studio.

And so we give thanks to God for the dear in-laws, or rather, as the Trumbull tribe would have said, the dear IN-LOVES. ᘒ

CHAPTER 31

THE
FAMILY
LETTERS

Of the tangible legacies my parents left us, nothing seems to me more remarkable than their letters—both the number and the content. How rich we were not to have been able to afford long-distance phone calls! Few families today have the permanent and intimately detailed record which now lies in a box in my attic—the complete set of Mother's letters to her children from 1954 through 1985. It is not unremarkable, I might add, that we also possess a great-great-grandmother's letters to her children, written more than a century earlier. I guess we're a crowd of hardened record-keepers.

As I have mentioned, Mother began to write to Phil and me twice a week in 1941 when we went away to school. I am sure there was never a week in her life from September of 1941 until she began to lose her mental powers in the mid-1980s, that she did not write to her children.

Mother's prayer, "Lord, send my children," began to see its fulfilment in April of 1952 when I went to Ecuador. The day before I was to sail she wrote:

My own dear Bets:
How inarticulate I feel at this moment, as I try to put into words my thankfulness to our Father for His good hand upon you over the years, for His faithfulness when I have been so

faithless, for His calling you into His service and giving you grace and faith to be obedient, for giving you courage when the way seemed hard, and utter and complete trust each step of the way. You have been *such* a comfort and very real help to me spiritually. I will miss being able to pour out my "woes" to you, dear, but how I do thank God for you and that He is leading you. As I write, a white throat [sparrow] is singing— one more reminder of *His* loving care!

At your leisure look up these verses and may they give you fresh courage and joy as you begin life under new and proba- bly difficult conditions: Deut. 1:17, 21, 29, 30, 31; Jer. 1:7–9.

As I said the other day, it is a comfort to me to know that Jim [Elliot, who was already in Ecuador] will be near you, but a much greater comfort to remember that "your life is hid with Christ in God"—the only safe place! God keep you, dear.

Loving you always, Mother.

P.S. This card [with a picture of Maine's rocky coast] re- minds me—"Who is a rock save our God?"

Phil and Margaret left for Northwest Territory, Canada, on February 10, 1953, where they served the Slave Indians, re- ducing their language to writing, under the auspices (later on) of the Northern Canada Evangelical Mission. Eleven days after Phil and Margaret left, Dave and Phyllis went to Costa Rica with the Latin America Mission.

In 1954 Jim went to Hampden DuBose Academy. By that time Mother had got herself a typewriter and set about using the hunt-and-punch method (with one finger on each hand), making at least five carbon copies. Jim wisely saved his cop- ies, returning them periodically to Mother, and she filed them. When copying machines became available she began copying all of our letters to her and sending them out, week by week, to all the rest. It was a fat package that we could look forward to—her letter, often with various enclosures, and several letters from siblings. We did not always manage to send her a letter a week, but usually at least two or three a month.

The family letter served to maintain a rare kind of unity between us when we had scattered to the four winds. We were bound together by it as we could not have been in any other way, and when Mother died we talked about giving it up. Nobody wanted to, so we still keep up with each other—not weekly, but probably six or eight times a year, making copies much more easily than Mother could.

How to give some idea of the flavor of our parents' family letters? With a thousand to choose from it's not easy, but here's a part of the first one Jim received, dated September 5, 1954:

> Beloved Children:
> That now includes our youngest, and I am having a hard time realizing that he is fourteen and actually on his way to HDA. Yes, he and Tom pulled out in true Howard style this morning a few minutes EARLY—around 7:25, in a big black lumbering bread truck [a donation to HDA from a Christian baker]. Jim was seated in one of the folding porch chairs beside Tom and in the back were Jim's trunk and suitcase and Tom's luggage and a blanket and pillow in case either of them gets sleepy. They are to stop for the night at motels as Tom will need his sleep . . .
> Dave, your letter telling of the general's visit was SO thrilling and we just devoured it . . .
> Phil and Margaret, your good letters came yesterday and also when we got home on Thursday we found the packages waiting for us. Jim was SO thrilled with his model dogsled and I am delighted with those wonderful moccasins . . . That grubstake certainly was interesting. Bets, how does it compare with what you used?

The letters were always conversational. What we wrote about Mother responded to. There was no doubt in our minds that she absorbed every word and remarked on things just as she would have done had we been sitting around the table together. In return, she expected commentary from us, and specific answers to her questions.

In April 1955, Ginny and Bud and their baby Kenny went to Palawan, Philippines, with the Association of Baptists for World Evangelism. On their departure Mother wrote,

> I have not let my mind dwell on the tokens of little Kenny's presence that are no longer here. A letter from Isobel Kuhn [author and missionary to China] telling of her parting from

[her daughter] Kathy has this word which helps me and may help Ginny and Bets: "The Lord showed me how I could use my head to help my heart. All lacerating thoughts should be avoided and heartrending scenes are not necessary. Plan the separation so as to keep the thoughts on other things . . . it is always hardest for the one left behind, for memory can claw at the heart." I feel I must clench my fist and make a firm face as Bets used to show us the way Phyllis did at PBI, or I might give way to tears. Guess I'd better get on to other things or they will be coming!

In February 1955, our parents visited Dave and Phyllis in Costa Rica and Jim and me in Ecuador just after the birth of our daughter Valerie. During this trip it was evident that something was amiss with my father. He was not his usual inquiring, eager, interested self. On returning home he had an encephalogram. Mother's letter reported:

There was an enormous brain tumor in the right frontal lobe. The doctor did not mince matters with me, but told me of the possibilities . . . a "golf ball" tumor which is not malignant, or a malignancy which puts out roots which cannot be completely removed and so is bound to return. Of course the other possibility is that the patient would die on the operating table. I am thankful to say that the Lord enabled me to face all of these possibilities by His grace with the one desire that HIS WILL should be done. Tom has been a pillar and stood by nobly though yesterday when he saw Dad just after the operation he turned a sickly green and had to vacate for a while. I, too, had to sit down by his bed and put my head down in order not to keel over.

Four days later she wrote, "I am so thankful to be near Dad and have so much to praise the Lord for. Billy [Scoville, Dad's cousin, who performed the operation] is just very pleased with Dad's quick recovery—he said it is the quickest he had ever seen from 'the biggest operation in the world.' "
In 1956 my husband, Jim (we had been married twenty-seven months), and four missionary colleagues were killed by Indians to whom they had meant to carry the gospel. Mother

wrote me a personal letter as soon as she heard the news by
shortwave. Here's an excerpt:

> How I long to take you in my arms and comfort you. As yet
> we have no official word as to the outcome. Rumors fly about.
> Well-intentioned people phone with the latest things from the
> radio or TV. The next one may completely contradict the one
> before. Hope rises and falls. But through it all God is giving
> unbelievable peace, not to ask that the boys be spared, but only
> that HIS perfect will may be accomplished and that you dear
> girls will be so wonderfully conscious of HIS strength and
> grace that you may be surprised at the peace of heart that He
> can give.
> The following quote from Amy Carmichael seems to fit:
> "Jonathan . . . does not so comfort David that he becomes
> necessary to him. He strengthened his hand in God. He leaves
> his friend strong in God, resting in God, safe in God. He de-
> taches his dear David from himself and attaches him to his
> Very Present Help. Then Jonathan went to his house, and
> David abode in the wood—WITH GOD."

The family letter was written two days later, when the final
word had come:

> Beloved Children: "The dead in Christ shall rise first . . .
> we . . . shall be caught up with them to meet the Lord . . .
> So shall we ever be with the Lord . . . Comfort one another
> with these words."
> Bets, my darling, perhaps even TODAY you will be with
> your dear one! May the hope of His coming be wonderfully
> precious and strengthening to us all. I can only say with Job
> "The Lord gave and the Lord hath taken away—BLESSED BE
> THE NAME OF THE LORD." He has promised that we "shall
> know hereafter" what He is doing, but till then let us "love
> Him, trust Him, praise Him." . . .
> All this past week of uncertainty, anguish, hope, despair,
> there has been a peace that has passed understanding, the
> promised grace which has been sufficient. Two words have
> been in my heart—"redeemed to God by Thy blood out of
> every kindred and tongue and people and nation." There
> MUST be some Aucas there—how my heart goes out to them
> in love and pity and longing that they may hear the word of
> hope, and how honored I feel to be the mother of six dear

children who all have the burden to take that Word to the ends of the earth. Let us unite in prayer for the Aucas, for the Slaveys, for those in Costa Rica and Palawan who do not know and are without hope.

And the other word that returned to me continually was that in Daniel 3:17, "Our God whom we serve IS ABLE . . . and will deliver (fear not them that kill the body) . . . BUT IF NOT . . . Though He slay me, yet will I TRUST HIM."

Two days later Mother wrote me another personal letter, telling of the many friends who were praying for me and for all the family, and of the outpouring of love they were experiencing. Then she added,

Of course we are wondering what you will do, dear. I have not written to urge you to come home for a time, as I know you know how dearly I would love to have you, but never for a minute would I want you to come unless you were sure it was God's will for you. I am sure that you will want to carry on, and I am right with you in that.

In March of that year Mother visited me again in the jungle. Mrs. DuBose, understanding Mother's longing to see with her own eyes that all was well with me, paid her way and accompanied her. My father took over for those few weeks the job of the family letter. He wrote,

"Betty, I have yours of February 23 and 28 and enjoyed so much your description of the little party you gave Valerie [her first birthday]. That was lovely! I think Mother will need some Kleenex, or fish around in her bosom for a small square of muslin."

He was being looked after at home by our much-loved helper of many years, old Mrs. Kershaw, who had lived in South Jersey all her life and had a unique way of expressing herself. Daddy could not resist giving us a few vignettes:

Mrs. Kershaw told me of a pigeon who used to come into a farm kitchen to be fed, got rather tame; but referring to the farm wife, Mrs. K. said, "She'd skite him out for fear he'd make some work around." An unusual euphemism!

When she was reminiscing about the farm where she had

lived, I asked, "Did you have an outside toilet?" "Oh yes, freeze to death out there"—with a sweep of the hand. "It was a nice little house though. It was a lovely toilet."

I miss you all a lot, but as I've said before, I'm so thankful to have you out on the firing line for God. Being alone, I've had special fellowship with Him lately, but don't think I don't need your prayers, for I do. The Devil never lets up as long as we are here.

A great deal of love to you all from your loving Dad.

Nearly all the family letters my father wrote describe the homey simple things he knew we all wanted to hear. But when he wrote to us individually he strengthened us in the Lord, as for example, when one of my brothers was living through an agonized period of doubt:

Your doubts are not so unusual. The best of men have had them, and I have noticed in many of the older writers that they were occasionally troubled with them. "Beloved, think it not strange concerning the fiery trial which is to try you, as though some strange thing happened unto you . . . your adversary the devil, as a roaring lion, walketh about, seeking whom he may devour: whom resist steadfast in the faith, knowing that the same afflictions are accomplished in your brethren that are in the world" (I Peter 4:12; 5:8, 9) . . . The Devil will always try to break down your faith in the Word and take it away from you; but remember that when Christ was terribly tempted in three ways in the desert, He quoted the Scripture three times, and only used His own words at the last, and the Devil was driven off . . .

We must stand on the fact that God's Word is true, it has stood the test of centuries, is still the best seller, and is powerful to strengthen us and help us meet temptation. Here's a verse from a fine hymn in the Keswick (England) hymnbook:

"Trust Him when dark doubts assail thee,
Trust Him when thy faith is small,
Trust Him when to simply trust Him
Seems the hardest thing of all."

. . . Now, just stand on the promises of God such as Isaiah 41:10, Psalm 55:22, Psalm 27:1 . . . Learn the old hymns and go over them in the night and when you are tempted. We are praying for you, and God loves you.

So do I. Your loving Dad.

As we have seen, Mother occasionally put her thoughts into verse. The following, entitled "The Comfort of the Scriptures to a Mother of Six," was, according to Mother's notation, "thought out at 3 a.m. on April 25, 1959":

I see him, Lord, in all that frozen waste,
A gallant figure pushing dauntless on,
The stinging snow and wind beat in his face—
I need Thy promise, Lord, to lean upon.
For Indian hearts are cold and icy too,
"A heart of flesh for stone," I hear Thee say?
And also, "He shall let my captives go!"
Now rest, my heart, in this sure Word today.

In steaming jungle, Lord, midst crawling life,
She labors patiently to tell Thy love,
Where naught is known save only human strife.
Whence comes my help if not from Thee above?
Arrows by day! Ah Lord, those Auca spears!
Thine angels charged to keep her? Yes, I know—
But, Lord, terror by night, loneliness and tears—
Yes, Lord, such rivers "shall not overflow."

And then another son, O God, so dear,
The opposition there is fierce and real;
The cunning black-robed hatred*—this I fear,
The foe is mighty, Lord, his heart is steel!
What was that whispered word? Greater art Thou?
The mighty God . . . all pow'r, shield and fortress!
In THEE I rest my troubled heart just now,
And find Thy Word my comfort in distress.

But Lord, those typhoons toss the little boat
Where still another daughter seeks to bring
To unreached peoples of those isles remote
The Word—"Christ died—He is thy Savior-King."

* There was strong persecution of Protestants by Catholics at that time in Latin America. Much has changed now.

What say'st Thou, Lord? (How kind He is to me!)
"E'en wind and sea obey Me. Peace, be still!
Through jagged coral reefs and weltering sea
I will be with her. Thou shalt fear no ill."

Two more are on my heart, Lord. These I bring.
Dear sons for whom Thou shedst Thy precious blood.
So quickly comes Thy Word (my heart would sing!)
"The steps of these are ordered of the Lord."
Imagination stayed on Thee, didst say?
Yes, only then can perfect peace be won.
Commit them unto Thee? Each night and day,
My Father, take them, keep them for Thine own.

During the summer of 1963 my parents sold the home in
Moorestown and moved to Vero Beach, Florida, where dear
friends, the Walter Buckinghams, had *given* them a house.
Daddy wrote a family letter on November 8, not dreaming it
would be his last:

Dear Family:
Once again I take my miniature Corona in hand to write you
the weekly letter. It is a glorious day here, with the mercury at
76 and a bright sun and blue sky, with a pleasant westerly
breeze. Mother and I passed our written tests this morning for
Florida drivers licenses, this afternoon she got our one license
plate at the Indian Rivah Cote House [his rendering of a Florida accent], I put it on the car, and now we are nearly Floridi-
ans . . . There are five letters and one note here from you,
which I'll answer seriatum.

He does just that, taking us in the order of our ages, com-
menting on each letter. He ends with an extract from an old
book, *The Old Gospel for the New Age,* by H. G. Moule:

(about Charles Simeon of Cambridge) "Day by day his earliest waking hours, won by brave self-discipline from sleep,
were spent, all through his life from young manhood onwards,
in solitary converse with God." Then about Ridley, a martyr:
"On October 16, 1555, at Oxford, on a morning of torrent rain
and fitful sunshine, at a stake set in Balliol ditch, in a fire
lighted with difficulty and delay, and which did its fierce work

only by degrees, died Nicholas Ridley, Bishop of London, late Bishop of Rochester, formerly Master of Pembroke in this University, crying with a wonderful great voice: *In manus tuas, Domine, commendo spiritum meum** till the fire touched the bag of gunpowder, and the cry was stilled."

End of paper. Must stop. Please excuse many mistakes. I read eagerly all of your letters, don't remember details of your work quite as well as Mother, who carried you all *under* her heart, but pray in detail for you all early every morning, and I do carry you *in* my heart and love you all. So interested in all you are doing.

Love to all, including grandchildren, from Dad and Grandpa.

On Christmas Day he and Mother were having breakfast. He turned to look over his left shoulder, which Mother thought strange, since he had no left eye. This happened several times, and when Mother asked why he said someone was there. He was so insistent that she finally walked with him around the little house, assuring him they were alone. They then walked over to the Buckinghams' house next door where they had been invited to open presents. As they reached the doorstep my father collapsed. Mrs. Buckingham heard Mother whisper, "Oh Lord, take him quickly and easily." He was taken to the hospital and died within an hour. Mother's family letter, written on January 1, begins with the Scripture, "O magnify the Lord with me and let us exalt His name together!"

How kind He has been to us in recent days! I can only thank Him continually for His goodness and mercy! It is just a week ago about this time that we were taking Dad to the hospital. I think I can say that he did not suffer at all . . . The most interesting thing about Dad's going was the way he kept looking over his shoulder and saying someone was behind him! Several have said that it was the Lord! . . .

When I heard that he was gone I could only feel a great sense of relief and rejoicing. FULLNESS OF JOY for Dad. Why should we be sad? (no rhyme intended!) Except for a few brief

---

* Into thy hands, Lord, I commend my spirit.

tears at the moment I heard, my heart has been free from anything but thankfulness.

Dad's will, drawn up in March of 1948, begins this way:

I, Philip Eugene Howard Jr., residing in Moorestown in the
state of New Jersey, do make and declare this to be my last
Will and Testament, revoking hereby all other wills heretofore
by me made.

I desire to bear testimony to my faith in the Lord Jesus Christ
as my personal Savior, believing that His blood cleanses me
from all sin; that He has gone to prepare a place for me, together with all other believers; that I have eternal life in Him;
and that I shall be raised bodily, with all other believers at the
second coming of Christ, and thereafter be forever with the
Lord.

I desire also to give thanks and praise from a full heart to
God, my Heavenly Father, for His abounding mercy and grace
to me all my life through; for my birth into a devout and happy
Christian home where I was trained by my dear Mother and
Father in the knowledge of God and His word; in giving me
great advantages with respect to education, travel, and friend-
ships; in giving me a dear, loving, and efficient wife, who has
borne me six dear children, and who has cheered, comforted
and helped me through all the years of our unusually happy
life together; in preserving me in many travels; in restoring me
in times of sickness; in protecting me in accidents; and allowing me to serve Him for many years. I look forward to
seeing my Savior face to face and to a joyous reunion with my
loved ones in Heaven.

The mail that poured in from all over the world was a fresh
revelation to us of the character of the man who had been our
father. There were letters from the small and the great, but
none from any greater, I think, than an old veteran missionary of West Africa, Miss Janet Miller, who had never met him
but had read *The Sunday School Times* for years. She wrote by
hand on airmail paper:

For the godly children of godly parents—
Never mind who I am; just a nobody, one of thousands who
found strength to meet impossible demands of a hard world

through the Word of God; led through the Bible by the [Sunday School] Times which revealed your father's undaunted spirit, the Christ who spoke through him . . . What a victor's crown he is wearing now! What a recompense he has received, beginning with the personally conducted journey with the One he felt behind him, who had conducted him through life and made him a blessing to thousands. In reading we heard not an editor but our Christ Jesus who spoke. And he was always more than ready to help individuals as his Lord did on earth, the weak and the infirm in body, mind, or spirit, full of sympathy. Do not trouble to answer. Only one of many. May his Christ be with you all.

Mother stayed in Florida for seven years. Her letters to us went on as always, and she spent her summers with me in New Hampshire. God gave her the privilege (and comfort) of mothering a group of younger women in a Bible class. We found an apartment for her in Massachusetts where Tom and Ginny and I, with our spouses, were all living. Later she moved into a suite in Tom's house, and after four years she chose to enter a retirement home in Quarryville, Pennsylvania.

Her course was finished on February 7, 1987. A part of a letter I wrote to family and friends who loved her tells the story:

She was up and neatly dressed in the morning (never in her life did she come to breakfast any other way), made it to lunch with the help of her walker, lay down afterwards, having remarked rather matter-of-factly to someone that she knew she was dying, and wondered where her husband was. Later in the afternoon cardiac arrest took her, very quietly.

Each of us (in chronological order) took a few minutes at the funeral to speak of some aspect of Mother's character. Phil spoke of her consistency and unfailing availability as a mother; of her love for Dad, ("He was always my lover," she said). I recalled how she used to mop her eyes at the table, laughing until she cried at some of my father's bizarre descriptions, or even at his oft-told jokes; how she was obedient to the New Testament pattern of godly womanhood, including hospitality. Dave talked about her unreserved surrender to the Lord, first of herself (at Stony Brook conference in New York), and then (painfully, years later at Prairie Bible Institute in Canada) of her children; of how, when we left home, she followed us not only with prayer but, with hardly a break for forty years, with a weekly letter. Ginny told how Mother's example taught her what it means to be a lady; how to discipline herself, her children, her home. Tom remembered the books she read to us (A. A. Milne, Beatrix Potter, *Sir Knight of the Splendid Way*, for example), and the songs she sang as she rocked each of us little children ("Hush, my baby, do not cry," "Go Tell Aunt Nancy"), shaping our vision of life. Jim pictured her in the small cane rocker in the bay window of her bedroom after the breakfast dishes were done, sitting quietly before the Lord with Bible, *Daily Light*, and notebook.

The last three years were sorrowful ones for all of us. Arteriosclerosis had done its work in her mind and she was confused and lonely ("Why hasn't Dad been to see me?" "He's been with the Lord for twenty-three years, Mother." "Nobody told me!"). Still a lady, she kept her shoes on, her nails manicured, always offered a chair to those who came. She had not lost her humor, her almost unbeatable skill at Scrabble, her ability to play the piano, sing hymns, and remember her children. But she wanted us to pray that the Lord would let her go Home, so we did.

The funeral ended with the six of us singing "The Strife is O'er," then all family members, including our beloved aunts Alice and Anne Howard, sang "To God Be the Glory." The graveside service closed with the doxology (the one with Alleluias). We think of her now, loving us with an even greater love, her poor frail mortality left behind, her eyes beholding the King in His beauty.

"If you knew what God knows about death," wrote George MacDonald, "you would clap your listless hands."

AFTERWORD

*T*hose who found this description of one man's family very different from the model they would wish to follow will probably not have gotten so far as to read the Afterword. Some may have read right through, finding principles which make sense which they would long to follow, yet feeling quite hopeless about doing so. To these I would repeat what I said in my Preface—this story is of *one* man's family, meant to be a description, not a prescription. The principles are sound and biblical, I believe. Their application will differ in different times and in different homes.

Be not dismayed! If you are convinced of the value of standards here set forth, never think of the impossible. *It is always possible to do the will of God.* Begin to be ready to do. What do you want your home to be? What does *God* want it to be? Waste no time wondering if you *can* do it. The question is simply *Will you?* Your weakness is itself a potent claim on the divine mercy (see 2 Cor. 12:10).

When David told his son Solomon that God had chosen him to build His house he encouraged him with these words, ''Be strong and courageous, and do the work. Do not be afraid or discouraged, for the LORD God, my God, is with you. He will not fail you or forsake you until all the work for the service of the temple of the LORD is finished'' (1 Chron. 28:20

NIV). Will not the same Lord be with any man or woman to whom He gives the task of building a home? Ask Him!

❦

When we climbed those mountains in New Hampshire, some of us would get tired sooner than others. There would always be one or two who would rush ahead and see the summit while the rest were still toiling upward. There would be a shout—"Come on! We're almost there! Wait till you see this view!"

Call Back

If you have gone a little way ahead of me, call back—
'Twill cheer my heart and help my feet along the stony track;
And, if perchance, faith's light is dim, because the oil is low,
Your call will guide my lagging course as wearily I go.

Call back, and tell me that He went with you into the storm;
Call back, and say He kept you when the forest's roots were torn;
That when the heavens thundered and the earthquake shook the hill,
He bore you up and held you when the very air was still.

O friend, call back and tell me, for I cannot see your face;
They say it glows with triumph, and your feet bound in the race;
But there are mists between us, and my spirit eyes are dim,
And I cannot see the glory, though I long for word of Him.

But if you'll say He heard you when your prayer was but a cry,
And if you'll say He saw you through the night's sin-darkened sky,
If you have gone a little way ahead, O friend, call back—
'Twill cheer my heart and help my feet along the stony track.

Mother sent me those lines, whose author she did not know, when I was a young mother. I was cheered by her call. It is my prayer that this story will be a "call back" to cheer others.

A Reading List for Parents

Abbott, John S. C. *The Mother at Home* (first published 1833). Grace Abounding Ministries, Inc., PO Box 25, Sterling VA 22170.

Alexander, J. W. *Thoughts on Family Worship* (1847). Soli Deo Gloria Publications, 213 W. Vincent St., Ligonier PA 15658.

Barnes, Robert G., Jr. *Who's in Charge Here?* Word Publishing, Waco TX. Avoiding the "power struggle" trap with your children.

Child, L. *The Mother's Book.* First published in Boston in 1831, now published by Applewood Books, c/o The Globe Paquot Press, 138 West Main Street, Chester CT 06412.

Colfax, David and Micki. *Homeschooling for Excellence.* Warner Books, New York NY. The authors' four sons were taught at home until they all entered Harvard.

Hendrick, Gladys West. *My First 300 Babies.* Janna Windsor, 335 Laurel Ave., Arcadia CA 91006, $9.95 in 1990. By a very wise midwife who had delivered 300 babies and helped the parents understand "It is not what the baby does—for at times he would seem unpredictable—it is what you do about it."

Prentiss, Elizabeth. *Stepping Heavenward* (1869). Grace Abounding Ministries, Inc., PO Box 25, Sterling VA 22170. Diary of a woman from age sixteen through marriage and motherhood—intimate, practical, delightful.

Ryle, John Charles. *The Duties of Parents* (1888). Christian Heritage Publisher, Box 719, Choteau MT 59422.

Theophan the Recluse. *Raising Them Right, A Saint's Advice.* Conciliar Press, Mt. Hermon CA.

Trumbull, Henry Clay. *Hints on Child Training* (1891). Wolgemuth and Hyatt Publishers, Brentwood TN.

Wilson, Ken. *The Obedient Child.* Servant Books, Ann Arbor MI. Children are not born obedient, they're trained.

Books on marriage:

Mason, Mike. *The Mystery of Marriage.* Multnomah Press, Portland OR. The best book I know on this subject.

Von Hildebrand, Alice. *By Love Refined, Letters to a Young Bride.* Sophia Institute Press, Manchester NH. She answers nearly every question a young bride could ask.